christian family
guide to

Married Love

Series Editor: James S. Bell Jr.

by Stephen R. Clark and Sybil A. Clark

ALPHA

A member of Penguin Group (USA) Inc.

International Standard Book Number: 1-59257-078-X
Library of Congress Catalog Card Number: 2003105467

05   04   03   8   7   6   5   4   3   2   1

Interpretation of the printing code: The rightmost number of the first series of numbers is the year of the book's printing; the rightmost number of the second series of numbers is the number of the book's printing. For example, a printing code of 03-1 shows that the first printing occurred in 2003.

Printed in the United States of America

Contents

Appendixes

Introduction

Married love—there is nothing like it! Only in married love do we truly reap all of the blessings that God has for his creation. All of God's children reap his blessings but only in the covenant of marriage can they all flow. Why? Because our sexuality is a gift from God, a blessing, part of his creation. The only protected sanctified place to fully express and enjoy our sexuality is within the marriage bond.

The ecstasy of orgasm with the one who is committed to loving us in holy matrimony is the closest experience of heaven that we will have while still on this earth.

While that means this book is all about a Christian couple's sex life, it's not just about sex. There's more to great sex in marriage than positions and technique. Great sex comes with a great foundation—a great marriage.

You will discover herein a wealth of information about sexuality, physical health, mental and emotional well-being, relationship management, and more, all from a biblical, Christian perspective. But the primary focus will be on how to enjoy great sex in your marriage and to spice up your sex life.

When we are obedient to God and follow his precepts, we avoid sex outside of marriage. We strive for sexual purity.

In this book you will discover very frank and honest descriptions regarding sex and the marital relationship. While we've been careful not to present material in an offensive or crude manner, some of the discussion, descriptions, and topics are presented in a very direct and graphic manner. We don't beat around the bush, because it's important to be honest and candid.

We understand that when one or both spouses have been sexually abused or had disturbing sexual experiences, their sexual functioning can become impaired. These couples are looking for answers. While this book may be helpful it is not written with abuse victims in mind and it may feel somewhat threatening.

Our intent is to provide you with useful, practical, and straightforward information about sex and marriage that you and your spouse can quickly benefit from. We hope what we have written blesses you and your marriage. There is so much peace, contentment, and satisfaction that we can attain in marriage. Learning how to sexually please your spouse and helping your spouse to sexually please you is all part of the pursuit of married love. There is nothing sweeter than having a smile on your face from the time you go to sleep until the time you wake up because you and your spouse had one of the most fantastic sexual nights you've ever known. We pray you will have many nights like this and truly enjoy this wonderful blessing that God has given to you and your spouse.

What's in This Book

In **Part 1, "In the Beginning,"** we take a look at what "comes naturally" regarding sex and what may not. It's important to understand who created sex and why. Sexual relations between a husband and wife are about much more than mere pleasure. We'll also examine some schoolyard stories and old wives' tales that may need to be cleared up.

After taking care of some of the preliminaries, in **Part 2, "The Fun Part,"** it's time to do it! First, though, you will learn a bit more about your body and your spouse's body.

In **Part 3, "All About Kids,"** we'll take a look at pregnancy, childbirth, and parenting, and how it all affects your sex life. We'll discuss privacy issues as well as the special challenges of blended families.

Finally, in **Part 4, "A Few Important Details,"** we'll take a look at issues outside the bedroom that can influence what happens inside the bedroom. We also discuss issues of faith, intimacy, health, and aging and how all of these affect the health of your marriage and the quality of your sex life.

Bonus Bits of Information

You'll also find these sidebars:

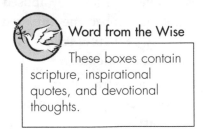

Word from the Wise

These boxes contain scripture, inspirational quotes, and devotional thoughts.

For Him

Here you'll find special bits of information, tips, instructions, and so on, targeted to men.

Dr. Truth

These boxes contain facts, advice, insights, informational highlights, tips, or other useful bits of biblically acceptable information related to sex and sexuality.

 ### For Her

In these boxes you'll find special bits of information, tips, instructions, and so on, targeted to women.

Part 1

In the Beginning

When it comes to sex, you will often hear that all that's required is doing what comes naturally. While there is a natural God-given attraction toward your spouse that finds an expression in sex, there are some things that you need to know. It's important to understand who created sex and why. Sexual relations between a husband and wife are about much more than mere pleasure. Although, the pleasure part is pretty cool and pretty important.

Whether you're about to get married for the first time or are getting married again, there are some considerations you should take a look at. Also, there were probably some school-yard stories about sex you picked up as a kid that need to be cleared up.

Coming Together as One

Why are you reading this book? Are you about to get married and are a tad clueless about what's supposed to happen in the bedroom? Maybe you've been married a few months and reality has overrun your expectations. Perhaps you've been married a few years and still feel that the sexual part of your relationship isn't working quite right. Maybe your previous marriage(s) had "bad sex," no sex, or "crazy sex." Perhaps what you learned of sex you learned before you became a Christian and you just want to know more about God's design for your sexuality and how it can be healthy, comforting, fun, and life giving within the covenant of marriage.

Regardless of why you're looking for information, you will find this book helpful. Whether you're an old married couple or about to be newlyweds, there's something for you here!

As you read this first chapter, you may wonder what some of this discussion has to do with sex. Hang in there and keep reading. There's more to good marital sex than body parts, positions, and pleasure points. Good sex needs a good foundation, so let's go back to the beginning.

In the Beginning

You've heard the story about Adam and Eve and the garden. That's where this sex thing got its start. "In the beginning God created ..." the earth, the heavens, the animals, the insects, and, well, everything! Creation is an amazing and awesome accomplishment. In seven days, the world came together as God, like an artist with an infinite canvas, painted life into existence. When he was done, he declared that it was good.

It's interesting that chapter 1 of Genesis takes a broad-brush approach, telling the entire story of creation in 31 verses. We learn how the planets, stars, plants, fish, birds, mammals, and all the rest came into being. But something really interesting happens around verse 26—the chronicle shifts focus, moving from the broad view to a specific recounting. The story moves from talking about *what* happened to focusing on *who* happened.

In the final six verses of chapter 1, the central "character" becomes humanity—men and women—a focus that carries through the rest of the Bible.

> "So God created people in his own image; God patterned them after himself; male and female he created them. God blessed them and told them, 'Multiply and fill the earth and subdue it. Be masters over the fish and birds and all the animals.' And God said, 'Look! I have given you the seed-bearing plants throughout the earth and all the fruit trees for your food. And I have given all the grasses and other green plants to the animals and birds for their food.' And so it was. Then God looked over all he had made, and he saw that it was excellent in every way. This all happened on the sixth day." (Genesis 1:27-31)

So what's the point? Simply that you, and all of humanity, are very special to God, and unique in all of his creation. You were created "in his own image"! You are "patterned" after God! You are "blessed"! You are "excellent in every way"! Understanding these truths and taking them to heart can directly improve the quality of your sex life with your spouse.

Word from the Wise

"And the LORD God said, 'It is not good for the man to be alone. I will make a companion who will help him.' ... Then the LORD God made a woman ... 'At last!' Adam exclaimed. 'She is part of my own flesh and bone! She will be called 'woman,' because she was taken out of a man.' This explains why a man leaves his father and mother and is joined to his wife, and the two are united into one." (Genesis 1:18, 22-24)

There is completeness when man and woman join together as one. It is part of Our Father's design.

There are several implications that come out of these six verses and that are reinforced throughout the Bible. First and foremost is that from the beginning, God intended for men and women to work together in a relationship to enjoy and manage the world he created. Second, since birth is only possible with the involvement of both a man and a woman, the coming together of one man and one woman in marriage is the only sexually intimate relationship ordained by God.

Adam and His Bride

How did Adam react when he first saw his new "bride"? He was quite excited and pleased!

"Now, although Adam and his wife were both naked, neither of them felt any shame." (Genesis 2:23-25) Isn't it a wonderful thought that a man and a wife could both just be naked together and feel no shame? You may be thinking that that doesn't exactly jibe with your own experience. In fact, for many Christians, the concept of nakedness and sexual relations is thoroughly muddied with tons of shame, embarrassment, and many misconceptions. So if God created males and females and ordained sex and called it good, what happened to mess things up?

One word: Sin.

When God placed Adam and Eve in the Garden, he provided everything they needed—they were denied no good thing. However, he did impose one, and only one, restriction:

> "The Lord God placed the man in the Garden of Eden to tend and care for it. But the Lord God gave him this warning: 'You may freely eat any fruit in the garden except fruit from the tree of the knowledge of good and evil. If you eat of its fruit, you will surely die.'" (Genesis 2:15-17)

You'd think this would be a piece of cake to handle. Adam and Eve had it all, and they had it all first. Everything around them was new. Even they were new! They had so much to explore and examine, and wonder and learn about. It should have taken eons for them to get bored, but apparently that wasn't the case. We don't really know how much time passed, but from the context it seems as if it didn't take long for things to go wrong.

Along came a serpent who slid up beside her and led poor Eve astray. The serpent, Satan in disguise, convinced her that it was no big deal to take a bite of the forbidden fruit. We don't know what that fruit really looked like. History and art have assumed it was an apple since it's easy to pick and eat an apple right from the tree. Whatever it was, Eve did what she wasn't supposed to do and then so did Adam.

What happened immediately after Adam ate the fruit? "At that moment, their eyes were opened, and they suddenly felt shame at their nakedness. So they strung fig leaves together around their hips to cover themselves." (Genesis 3:7)

From that point on, things got really squirrelly between men and women. Not only that, but all of creation—every molecule, DNA strand, atom, microbe, element, and cell—lost its inherent goodness as sin spread its deadly infection over and into everything. Nothing in God's creation went untouched or unaffected by sin.

When confronted by God, what did Adam and Eve do? How did they feel? They covered themselves with fig leaves and tried to hide from God. Of course, God already knew what sin had occurred. Unfortunately, Adam and Eve played the blame game, trying to avoid personal responsibility and accountability. They had a choice and they made the wrong one. Afterward, they had opportunities to come clean and maybe even set things right again. They didn't. From that point on life became hard and messy.

The Aftermath

And that's where we are today—still dealing with the messiness. One area that sin really affects is sex. Sin has terribly distorted and dirtied sex. In the garden, when God sought out Adam, Adam told God that he was afraid because he was naked. God's response was "Who told you that you were naked?" (Genesis 3:10) This feeling of shame is not what God wanted for his creation. Sexual intimacy, the way God created it, is supposed to be (and still can be) something beautiful and worshipful. Unfortunately, too many people still feel shameful and think of their sexual experiences as ugly, painful, and abusive.

Instead of intimacy being confined to a married relationship between an adult man and woman, every kind of sexual coupling occurs inside and outside of marriage. Even within Christian marriages, because our values have been so warped by worldliness, misconceptions and sinful behavior have crept in. Spouses force spouses to engage in improper and lewd behavior, wrongly believing that just because they're married it's okay. Much of the wrong or immature thinking regarding sex among Christians is due to the failure of Christian pastors, educators, leaders, and parents to openly talk about sex in a truly biblical context.

Perhaps you grew up in a Christian home where sex was a taboo topic that was never really discussed. It was viewed as dirty. Then you went through puberty and sex was on your mind all the time—which made you feel dirty or ashamed, only you weren't sure why. Or maybe you grew up in a home where your dad had a stash of *Playboy* magazines and was always making crude remarks that both titillated and confused you.

As Christian parents, we need to learn how to raise our children with healthy views about sexual abstinence before marriage and the wonder and delight of sex within marriage. The more you learn, the more you can teach your kids.

Hopefully, regardless of what kind of home you grew up in or what your parents told you about sex, over time and on your own, you've learned enough truth that your attitude toward sex is one of respect and wonder. You know it's something special and ordained by God, otherwise you wouldn't be here. And now, you want to gain an even better and healthier understanding.

Good for you! You're on the right track!

The Blessings of Marriage (and They Do Exist)

If you've watched just about any sitcom on TV that involves characters who are married, it's easy to get a distorted view of marriage. Too often the husband is portrayed as a clueless dunce, the wife is a shrew, and the kids are little smart-alecky geniuses who always know better than mom and dad. The husband is always after sex and the wife is always avoiding sex, and often both use sex as a tool for negotiating something they want from the other. Intrusive in-laws, nosey co-workers, and annoying relatives all add to the chaotic depiction of marriage and family life. Lust, infidelity, premarital sex among the kids, and more are commonly portrayed as just part of "normal" life.

It's easy to forget that sitcoms are both gross exaggerations and over-simplifications of reality, which is why they are (sometimes) funny. They are not reality and they are not models for good Christian marriages. Thank God! Marriage and families are far richer experiences than any TV sitcom or movie can even begin to depict.

Marriage is a wonderful thing, and not just because you get to have sex. In fact, sex is more wonderful in marriage because that's where it's supposed to happen. It's one of many critical threads that make marriage one of life's most beautiful tapestries of experience.

Why did God create Eve after creating Adam? So that Adam would not be alone and so that he would have someone to help him through life. Marriage is about companionship, sharing, mutual support, and intimacy. The exclusiveness of sexual relations with your spouse seals your relationship and sets it apart from all others. The vulnerability and nakedness experienced in sexual relations harkens us back to the innocence of the Garden when Adam and Eve were naked and unashamed.

Among the many blessings of marriage, for some what could be the most significant is that it brings an end to all the complexities and heartbreaks of dating. In marriage, you now have someone you can cherish who will always cherish you, even on a bad hair day. Getting a pimple or having occasional bad breath are minor inconveniences rather than devastating embarrassments. Never again do you have to worry about having a date for New Year's. Never again do you have to wonder if he's going to ask you out, or work up the nerve to call her for a date. What a relief!

A True Mate

While you probably have many friends, it's hard to know more than a couple really well, or for them to know you really well. In marriage, you have one person you can focus on and get close to, and let yourself be known to, without the barriers of time or distance. You can count on each other and always be there for each other. At the end of a long, hard day, it can be extremely comforting knowing you have an intimate companion—a loving husband or wife—to come home to. You have a mate.

For Him

Wow! You've found your mate, your missing rib! Work with her, consider her, cherish her, remember her, and please her. It's a life-long investment with life-long dividends. But remember, life is in the living—make every day count.

Still, being with the same person, and so vulnerable day in and day out, can be intimidating. At times, you will feel the urge to push away and be alone. This is normal and actually a good thing. All human beings need privacy and periods of time alone. Sex keeps these periods from going on too long in marriage.

The Goal of Marriage

Whether you're married or not, you've probably been to or even involved in a wedding. What an ordeal! It can take months, or even years to plan one, and it's all over in a matter of minutes or a few hours.

The preparation for our marriage starts when we're kids. Both boys and girls play house and pretend to be moms and dads (and sometimes both play doctor!). Girls might play with dolls and boys might play at being a fireman or policeman. Girls want to marry their dads. Boys want to marry their moms. For most, there's the awareness early on that being married is a good and desirable thing.

As we grow up in our bodies, we also grow up in our outlook toward the opposite sex (there's that word!) and begin viewing them differently. Some of this has to do with them beginning to look differently—girls get new curves and boys get lanky and muscular and sound funny. Interests grow, attractions draw us toward someone, and you start talking and passing notes and holding hands. *Voilá*—you're a boyfriend or a girlfriend. Then the teasing begins for the guys and the wedding talk starts for the girls, followed in not too many years by dating, kissing, and all the complications of romance and young love.

Through all of this, in the back or forefront of our minds, there is a certainty or the hope that one day you will be a part of your own family, married with kids, till death do you part, for better or for worse. And threading all of the growth, awkwardness, development, wonder, curiosity, and hormone surges is this thing called sex. It is because our sexuality is so obvious to us from early on, and the changes in our bodies are so dramatic, that it becomes easy to divorce the idea of sex from the concept of marriage and relationship.

Sex too often becomes nothing more than a drive that takes on a life of its own, whether marriage is involved or not. Today, sex is viewed most often as just another bodily function or a sporting activity, a need that must be met, a release that has to be eased whenever and however an individual wants. This view is shared by men and women alike. It is not what God intended, either in or out of marriage.

Our culture and society are permeated with sin-affected views and opinions, many that "sound good" but are in reality not biblical, and not healthy for Christians to adopt. Yet, because of the subtlety of these ideas, Christians are indeed affected (infected!) by the world's wrongheadedness, particularly in the area of sex. Carried into a marriage, these wrong sexual ideas can breed disaster.

The point of marriage is not just to "score" legitimate sex. Rather, sex is an important element that legitimizes and

For Her

Cherish him, think of him, hear him, pay attention to what makes him feel valued, involve him. He chose you because he loved you. He made a life-long commitment to you. Work with him, enjoy him, laugh with him, love with him.

seals a marriage. It is not the point of marriage, yet healthy sex is critical to the success of every marriage.

Dr. Truth

> When God put Adam and Eve in the Garden of Eden it was a beautiful thing. Together they were one. Make a Garden of Eden in your home. Make yourselves a place in your marriage where you can truly experience the love and unity that God desires for your marriage. When you sin, repent, reconcile with each other, forgive each other, and let the goal of each moment of discord be to come back together to the Garden where Father intended for you to be.

Two Can Feel Like a Crowd!

If you've lived alone for a time and had full control over your own space, getting married can crowd your lifestyle. You have far less privacy and someone is always expecting to know where you are and what you're up to. Where you put your dirty towel, how you manage your sock drawer, and what you keep in the refrigerator are all subject to someone else's input and opinions.

Going to bed holds its delights, but also requires some adjustments. Suddenly, it matters if you snore, stay up late or rise early, prefer the left side of the bed, toss and turn throughout the night, and so on. All of this plays into what happens when you have sex, since most sex tends to happen in bed.

Getting married and working through all of the mundane, nit-picky idiosyncrasies of our humanity takes time, tolerance and tenacity. Indeed, we do need to find understanding, agreements, and compromises so that we can *live* together as God intended, not just to *survive* living together.

The Purpose of Marriage, With or Without a Brood

We started off in the Garden of Eden, together, male and female. We left our fathers and our mothers to come together in unity. Our marriage together is a reflection of who God is. Our creation and the covenant of marriage came from the heavenly places as Father and Son decided on our making. Our goal in life is eternity with Father, Son, and Holy Spirit in the heavenly places.

When we think of marriage we have to ask, in the long haul, where and how will it end? Now that we're together, what's the goal? The goal is a well-lived life together, (with or without children).

Married life gives us the opportunity to have a little glimpse, a little piece of heaven, before we get there. What will we have in heaven that we could start having right here?

We learn a little about this from Jesus' time on earth. Jesus listened to his Father, spent time with his Father, "knew" what his Father was doing. You could say that there was a heavenly communion going on between Father and Son, even though they were apart. Jesus went off alone many times just to pray. What is prayer but talking with Father God?

People who have reported life after death experiences claim to have "in their spirit" been in the heavenly places. They report a type of ecstasy there, an incredible "feeling" that goes beyond words.

An Encounter with Ecstasy

The Tanakh, a modern Jewish translation of the Old Testament, uses the word "ecstasy" to describe Saul's encounter with the Spirit of God in 1 Samuel 10:6: "The spirit of the Lord will grip you, and you will speak in ecstasy along with them, you will become a new man." Christians translate the word as "prophesy." ("… the Spirit of the Lord will come upon you with power, and you will prophesy with them. You will be changed into a different person.")

Considering the context, the Jewish translation seems to be more fitting. The point is, when the spirit of God comes on us it is a supernatural encounter. The Jews understood this unity with God as ecstasy. Similar to the ecstasy of making love to your spouse!

Orgasm is the most intensely physical experience a human being can have. This ecstasy was created for us by our Heavenly Father out of who he is, out of the heavenly realm. This moment of orgasm together, this moment of ecstasy in his creation, I believe, is the closest we can come on earth to experiencing a piece of heaven.

Both Jesus' relationship with his Father and the beautiful design of their creation provides us a glimpse of what the outcome of marriage is. Marriage is the lifelong relationship of knowing each other, hearing each other, hiding away to talk with each other, being known by another in an intimate way, seeing what the other is doing, living in the real world and dealing with the real world both separately and together and, for moments of time, feeling the presence of heaven in the ecstasy of orgasm.

A Godly Marriage

The outcome of marriage is to grow old together peacefully, to work through life's struggles, personal struggles, and marital struggles on a day to day basis so that each day can finish and a new day can begin. The outcome of marriage is to nurture each person as an individual and to commune together as a couple, so that when life draws to an end there are no regrets and no shame. The outcome of marriage is to have satisfaction of a life lived, in Christ, before God, together and to have great joy in who God created us to be and having found the missing part of ourselves in each other.

> **Word from the Wise**
>
> "Then God said, 'Let us make people in our image, to be like ourselves. …' So God created people in his own image; God patterned them after himself; male and female he created them." (Genesis 1:26-27)
>
> Women and men are incomplete without each other. Marriage of one man and one woman, in unity, speaks forth the image of God.

Ecstasy in our human lives is found in the orgasmic unity within a covenanted relationship of marriage that involves every aspect of our being: mind, body, soul and spirit. Ecstasy is what we will experience in heaven for all time as we commune with our Heavenly Father: mind, body, soul and spirit.

A marriage needs time for intimacy: emotional, intellectual, and physical. We need to commune with our spouse. Sexual intimacy and taking time for each other deepens and enriches our marital life. Find time to deepen this part of your marriage.

Chapter 2

Debunking the Myths

Learning about sex is usually hit and miss—and myth! You picked up tidbits from school buddies, overheard bits of conversation between your parents and other adults, sneaked peaks at the naughty section of the bookstore, and saw some questionable stuff on television. All this gets mixed in with the formal education that comes in school and in "the talk" with mom and dad.

Often, this mishmash of information leads to a great deal of confusion and the generation of wrong "facts" that can trip you up in the bedroom.

Heather's Story

Heather was college educated, in her mid-twenties, intelligent, and very competent in her mid-level position with a large, global corporation. And she was getting married! She was excited and spent months in preparation. Her fiancé, Tim, worked for the same company as a senior computer technician. Both were a little geeky and very career oriented. They weren't planning to have children for at least the first few years.

The wedding was held in a small stone chapel on a crisp fall day. All went well and the happy couple took off to Hawaii for a two-week honeymoon. Back home and back at work, Heather brought in all of their photos and settled into her routine.

After a few weeks, something began to happen. Heather was feeling a bit odd. Her co-workers, concerned, asked her if all was okay. Hesitantly, Heather shared that she'd just found out she was pregnant. Everyone was happy for her, but stunned. One friend said, "But I thought you and Tim didn't want kids so soon."

"We didn't," Heather replied.

"What happened?" asked the co-worker. "You did use birth control didn't you?"

"No," replied Heather. "I didn't think you could get pregnant when you're under stress and I was really stressed out with the wedding and all!"

Her friends did their best not to laugh too hard at her naiveté. But Heather is not alone. Probably everyone has picked up some bit of misinformation touted as fact. How do these little gems get formed?

The actual "truth" about the stress/pregnancy issue is this: When a woman is under excessive stress it is possible that her body will delay ovulating for up to two weeks. Many women have had periods two weeks late. So, while stress can't prevent pregnancy, stress can delay ovulation.

Whenever you encounter a piece of "wisdom" that seems a bit odd, check it out. Ask your doctor or check a medical or other reputable reference. Be careful what you pick up from the Internet, too. The Internet has become a veritable cauldron of overcooked bad information.

Old Wives' Tales

What are some of the more typical old wives tales? Here are a few:

Douching with vinegar after sex will keep you from getting pregnant. There are variations on the ingredients, including using a popular soft drink! It makes no difference what you douche with after having sex, you can still become pregnant. Once a man has ejaculated any amount of sperm into your vagina, the race is on. Almost instantly a substantial number of sperm are well out of reach of any douching you might do.

Additionally, douching is generally not recommended for any reason. The vagina is delicate and designed to be self-cleansing. Douching can upset the balance of natural and healthy bacteria and actually increase the chances of infections.

You cannot get pregnant having sex during your period. While the chance of pregnancy may be less during menstruation, it is not zero. You can still become pregnant.

The reason women can get pregnant during menstruation is that sperm can live up to 7 days. Women ovulate 14 days before the first day of menstruation. If a woman has a

28-day cycle, she ovulates 14 days before her first day of menstruating (and 14 days after her first day of menstruation). If a woman menstruates for 7 days and has sex on the 7th day of menstruation, and the sperm live 7 days, then the sperm could be alive when ovulation occurs. *Voilá*, pregnancy. Women who have a 21-day menstrual cycle ovulate on their 7th day of menstruation. If sperm enter the vagina from day one of menstruation and live 7 days, they may still be alive during ovulation. *Voilá*, pregnancy.

Having sex before you've had your first period will not result in pregnancy. It's sad that in today's society this is even an issue. Unfortunately a growing number of girls are having sex at younger and younger ages. They do so believing they can't get pregnant, and then they do.

The reason you can get pregnant before you begin to menstruate is this: girls never know when they will begin to menstruate. This also means that they don't know when they first ovulate. Since ovulation comes 14 days before menstruation, if girls have sex before menstruation, they might be having sex during ovulation and voilá, pregnancy. Back in the old days, girls generally started menstruating between the ages of 12 and 16. Today many girls are menstruating at 8 and 10 years of age. There is great risk of pregnancy for girls before menstruation begins.

Even though adults are the main audience for this book, we include this fact in the event a young girl is reading to learn more. And to arm you when you become a parent so you can provide accurate information to your children. The bottom line is, virtually any time you have sex, you can get pregnant.

For Her

Be careful how you handle your man's parts. The penis can generally endure intense stimulation, which most men prefer. However, the tip of the penis is very sensitive, and rubbing it the wrong way can be painful and annoying. Also, the testicles are extremely sensitive and must be handled with extreme care. The slightest bump to the testicles can bring the biggest man to tears. Grasp the penis firmly, but handle the testicles gently.

If he wears a condom she won't get pregnant. Couples who use condoms as their primary form of birth control have almost always had at least one or more experience of condoms breaking during intercourse, slipping off in the vagina during intercourse, or slipping off while her husband is withdrawing. These become uncertain moments for the couple trying to avoid pregnancy.

I'm 37, I've been using a diaphragm for 16 years and haven't gotten pregnant yet. Maybe I actually can't get pregnant. One woman truly thought she was infertile for awhile. But then, along came a little girl. Women can have babies at later ages of life. Until a woman is totally through menopause, she can still get pregnant.

The pill will stop me from getting pregnant. One doctor told of a woman who was absolutely shocked when he told her she was pregnant. Her response was, "Well, I took the pill just like I was supposed to, one on the first of every month!" Where did she get this idea? Someone, not the doctor, had seriously misinformed her and she didn't bother to read the instructions that came with the pills.

Nice people only do it once a month and really nice people don't do it that often. This is what a lot of nice Christian girls have been told in years past. How often you have sex has nothing to do with how nice you are or aren't. The old myth would almost have women believe that they should maintain celibacy after marriage. It was these sorts of messages that caused young women to feel guilty and uptight if they enjoyed sex or had it too often; this meant there was something wrong with them. How sad that the church has given people these sorts of messages. God's wonderful gift to married couples has been squashed by his own people.

You can get a sexually transmitted disease (STD) from public toilets. The truth is, most organisms (including STD organisms) can only survive a short time in the air, as on a toilet seat. Second, these organisms have to come in direct contact with your vagina, urethra, anus, or open cut or wound on your legs and there must be enough of the germs alive and present to make you sick. This is extremely unlikely. Sexually transmitted diseases are transmitted by, well, sexual activity and the exchange of bodily fluids. They need the moisture and warmth to stay alive.

Word from the Wise

"Jesus said to the people who believed in him, 'You are truly my disciples if you keep obeying my teachings. And you will know the truth, and the truth will set you free.'" (John 8:32)

When Jesus tells us the truth will set us free, he means *all* truth, including truth about reproduction and sexual relations. When we know the truth we don't have to live in unreasonable fear.

Old Husbands' Tales

Just as girls and women tend to have their own repertoire of falsehoods, men and boys have a few falsies they cling to as well (sorry about the pun). Here are some of their favorites:

Withdrawing the penis before ejaculating will prevent pregnancy. Men generally don't like dealing with birth control, especially when it comes to having to wear a condom. Even though many modern condoms are far more sensitive and comfortable than the early models, they can reduce the man's pleasure. So many men try to avoid them altogether and promise to withdraw their penis before ejaculating. Or they promise to put on a condom after enjoying several minutes of unprotected sex. Either way this doesn't work, except by chance.

First, even before orgasm men secrete pre-ejaculatory fluids that aid in lubrication and that contain sperm. It only takes one sperm to cause pregnancy. Second, orgasm can come on fast or slow, and in the heat of passion, reason flees. The odds are very high that the man will either pull out after he begins to ejaculate, or not pull out at all.

Using a condom every time will protect from disease and pregnancy. Wrong again. Condoms are not 100 percent effective. And the chance of that condom you keep stored in your wallet or car being defective is really high. While manufacturers strive for the highest quality standards, defects can and do occur. Condoms can have holes and it only takes a tiny, microscopic hole to provide an escape hatch for eager sperm or virus. Also, rubber and latex break down over time, especially if exposed to heat and cold. Condoms kept for long periods of time are not as reliable as newly purchased ones.

Wearing tight underwear will make me unable to impregnate a woman. Ouch! Wearing tight underwear will make you very uncomfortable and may reduce your sperm count, but it will not render you infertile. Again, it only takes one sperm to do the job. If you and your wife are having trouble getting pregnant, your doctor may advise wearing boxers instead of briefs. This is because sperm are very temperature sensitive, which is why the testicles hang down outside the body.

Bike riding can hurt my potency. This seems to be true for men, but it depends on how much time you spend riding a bike. Both men and women can have trouble with both orgasm and urination after extended cycling. The pressure point for men lies directly on the artery supplying blood to the penis and can indeed affect their potency. Impotency can be short- or long-term, depending on the frequency and duration of riding; long-distance bikers risk the possibility of becoming impotent permanently. If you are a cyclist, consult your urologist about "safe" cycling. Maybe check out a wide-bottom seat to spread your weight around!

I can enlarge my penis in weeks if I take the right pill! Sorry guys, only surgery can enlarge your penis permanently. Pills, pumps, and exercises don't have the effect of surgery, which can lengthen the penis by an inch or widen it (by injecting body fat or doing dermal grafting). However, the American Urology Association says surgery doesn't necessarily work and isn't necessarily safe. The lengthening surgery can leave you with a downward-pointing penis that wobbles during sex; the fat injections can move around under the skin and leave you looking lumpy. If you're concerned about your penis, see a Board Certified Urologist to get your questions answered.

A man can fracture his penis. This is actually true. It's possible for a man to fracture his penis if he hits it hard against his wife's pubic bone or runs into a wall or something while his penis is erect. If this happens, immediate medical attention is necessary. The damage can be repaired but it needs to be tended to quickly.

For Him

Be gentle with your wife, whether in touching her body or hearing her share something she sincerely believes is true that you know is not. Whatever you do, don't laugh, at least not at first. Let her talk, then suggest that there might be a different view, or that that's not what you've heard. Look it up together in a book. When the truth surfaces and she is able to laugh at herself, then you can laugh, gently, with her. Never ridicule or make fun of your spouse. You don't know it all either.

Tales Told In School

In a sixth-grade class, one boy became upset in the classes on reproduction. When the teacher explained where babies came from he was mad and told the teacher she was wrong. He went on to adamantly tell the class that his mother told him she had ordered him out of a catalog! Of course, the kids in the class laughed. He was embarrassed but trusted his mother so much that his real sentiment was anger that the class was being lied to.

Joan recalls how the girls tried to enlarge their breasts through a special exercise. "We were told that if we grabbed hold of our forearms with the opposite hand, held our arms up straight in front of us, squeezed our hands around the opposite forearm and pushed forward repeatedly, that our breasts would get bigger. What we didn't know then was this is an exercise to strengthen the pectoral muscles but wouldn't increase breast size."

I also remember hearing about an ad in the paper where you could send $10.00 for the "key" to breast enlargement. What they sent people for their money was a picture of a hand. They were told that massaging their breasts would cause them to enlarge. This isn't true either.

Almost every schoolyard gossip line promoted the idea that you can get pregnant just by kissing. Some modified that to kissing only after you got married. And of course the classic about somehow getting pregnant from just swimming with boys in the same pool! No one stopped to think that sperm couldn't survive in chlorinated water.

You must have your own stories from the past. (Did a stork bring you to your parents or did they find you in the cabbage patch?) If there are "truisms" about sex that you're not sure of, do some research. Either ask your doctor if the information is accurate or go to an online medical site to see what you can find.

Never Assume

When sifting through your accumulated knowledge, exercise wisdom and caution. As we've shown, some of the knowledge you've picked up in school, in life, in church, and in your home can be flawed. When it comes to sex and a healthy marriage, you can't afford to act on inaccurate information. Doing so could hurt you and your spouse.

A lot of people are ready to provide endless nuggets of advice to young couples struggling with being newly married and to older couples having problems getting pregnant. Just as scripture cautions you to test prophecy, so should you test advice. If it sounds hokey or odd, or if the suggestion makes you uncomfortable, don't act without checking the facts.

Dr. Truth

Ever heard "There's no such thing as a dumb question"? If you think your question is dumb you may feel too self-conscious or embarrassed to ask it. When I have these questions for my medical professional I start with "I know this seems like a dumb question but ...." Don't live with information that could be faulty. Let yourself hear it from an expert.

Consider the source. Is your spinster Aunt Millie the one telling you to eat more green vegetables right before bedtime with the shades drawn and a candle burning in the room? Or maybe it's your Casanova bachelor college buddy who's advising you to sit in a pan of iced mineral water for 30 minutes and drink a cup of red wine mixed with vanilla before having sex to improve, or decrease, your sperm count?

Talk to each other, and be kind. A key ingredient to a great sex life is good communication. (Actually, it's a key ingredient to a lot of good things, including a great marriage!) You both know a lot of the right stuff about sex, and you both have some misconceptions. By sharing what you know you can educate each other. But be sensitive as you share. Don't laugh at each other's absurdities. Listen, be gentle, and be willing to have your assumptions challenged in some areas.

Word from the Wise

"Be humble and gentle. Be patient with each other, making allowance for each other's faults because of your love. Always keep yourselves united in the Holy Spirit, and bind yourselves together with peace." (Ephesians 4:2-3)

Living the truth of this scripture is more important in marriage than in any other setting because your flaws are on parade 24/7!

Chapter 3

First Time Married

Did you know sex and marriage could be compared to a new car? Think about it! Before you buy a new car, you look around at all the options. Every time you see certain models, you practically drool as you imagine what it would be like to be behind the wheel. Then you go shopping and take a few on test-drives, carefully weighing the pros and cons of each. Finally, you make your decision and commit. You slide into your brand new car and the first thing you notice is that new car smell. Ahhhhh.

The next thing you do is try to figure out where all the controls are and what each button, knob, or switch does. It may actually take you a few days to sort everything out. But soon you're cruising along merrily with the air conditioning set just right and the radio tuned to your favorite station.

Getting married for the first time will present you with a whole new set of "buttons, knobs, and switches"! Learning how things work is essential, particularly in the bedroom. Given the high expectations of that first night, what is supposed to be romantic can actually be tense, frustrating, or disappointing.

Shyness Can Be a Virtue

You get to your wedding night suite, tired from the long day. You are both excited and nervous about what's supposed to happen. Since you're not used to undressing in front of someone else, it feels a bit awkward. The beautiful bride goes into the bathroom to freshen up and change while the husband undresses and gets under the covers. Eventually, the bride emerges in her brand new sexy nightie and very quickly joins her man. Both are a bit shy and not quite sure what to do next. Neither wants to appear too reticent or offend the other, but both are feeling a bit strange, yet really turned on!

Recognize that it's okay to be shy, especially on that first night. In fact, a little coyness now and then can actually be sexy. On your first night together it's to be expected. So talk to each other. You may find that after all the activity of the day you are both flat-out exhausted and in need of a good night's rest. That's okay. Sex will be much better in the morning. A lot of people prefer sex in the morning.

Whatever you do, do it in agreement and love. If one of you wants to try to go for the sex and the other one doesn't, drop it. It won't be fun or enjoyable if one of you just wants to go to sleep.

You Can Wait Until Tomorrow

If it's late enough and the day has been exhausting enough, you might be feeling just too tuckered to pucker. Exhaustion can have that effect on your sex drive. Sometimes it's just not there when you wish it were.

If so, cuddle up next to each other, and sit in each other's arms, sip some wedding wine, and talk about your day. Relax and decompress. Don't rush or force your spouse or yourself. Rub each other's backs, arms, legs, and whatever! Maybe what you both need is a nice long hot bath, together. Get a room with a tub for two—you won't regret it.

As you relax together and de-stress, you may discover renewed energy which can lead to passion. Set aside the expectations, realizing that you both need some time to let your shyness settle down. Also keep in mind that if sex doesn't happen that first night, you've still got a lifetime of nights ahead of you.

However, if after a few days sex isn't happening because your spouse is refusing, or trying but having pain or penetration problems, you need to get to a therapist. Something's wrong and needs to be addressed. Don't force your spouse to have sex as that will only make the situation worse. Be sensitive and loving.

Many men and women who were abused as children or young adults experience painful memories in a sexual situation, even in marriage. Some women have problems with their vaginas not opening up to receive a penis and penetration is impossible. She may not discover this until the wedding night. If this is the case, she will need time, love, prayer, and understanding to remove the blocks. You may also need some pastoral counseling, receiving prayer and support from those who don't want evil to get a foothold in your lives.

It's Okay to Fumble

Let's assume you and your spouse have got a second wind and are full of energy. Woohoo! Let the good times roll! As you come together with energy on your side, you still need to exercise some caution. You are about to make love, not jump each others' bones. Sex for Christians has the potential to be a very worshipful act. You are coming together truly as one, making yourself vulnerable, allowing yourself to be naked before your lover. Be kind, considerate, and polite. But it's okay to fumble, too!

If you are both very naïve about the opposite sex you may want to start with basic exploration. Your spouse may never have seen a naked body. If your embarrassment factor is low, invite your spouse to "window shop" your body (this works both ways). Take a good look, ask questions. If the embarrassment factor is high and you have to hide under the covers you might only be comfortable enough to kiss and hug. Remember, don't push. Everything comes in its own good time.

As you explore one another's bodies and engage in actual intercourse, it's possible to get hurt, physically or emotionally. For example, if your wife is taking an exploratory trip around your testicles, she may not know what effect certain kinds of touching may have. The same is true as your husband explores your body; he may not know what it's like for you to have your breasts/nipples touched in certain ways, or your vaginal areas. He might cause you a little pain without knowing it. Emotionally, you may start feeling intruded upon during bodily exploration. Both of you need to let the other person know what is happening while maintaining a sense of humor and being readily forgiving. Allow each other to make mistakes and talk about them.

 For Him and Her

There may be a time when a little roughness with your breasts can be a turn-on, so you need to let your husband know that "right now" your nipples are too sensitive for how he's touching your breasts. Let him know that this could change in 5 minutes or tomorrow, though, so it's not that he shouldn't ever touch you like that, just not now.

What Works for Me

As you'll learn more and more, don't just tell your spouse what doesn't work, tell your spouse what *does* work for you and your body.

Not every woman understands exactly how sensitive a man's testicles are. It can be a real turn-on for the woman to touch them gently, or even kiss or suck them. But gentleness is the word here. The same holds true for men when they're caressing the woman. Not every man knows or understands that a woman can prefer very gentle stimulation of her clitoris one day, and maybe want it to be a little more aggressive the next. To be safe, start gently and then ask.

In every act of lovemaking, if you're not sure what your husband or wife prefers, ask. You may have to ask every time you make love because it can vary. Both men and women can have a shift in mood.

For Him

If your wife squeezes your testicles a little too firmly, quickly but kindly let her know that makes you uncomfortable. Let her know the kind of touch that is better for you.

Word from the Wise

"'Oh, how delightful you are, my beloved; how pleasant for utter delight! You are tall and slim like a palm tree, and your breasts are like its clusters of dates.' I said, 'I will climb up into the palm tree and take hold of its branches. Now may your breasts be like grape clusters, and the scent of your breath like apples.'" (Song of Songs 7:6-8)

Whoever said there wasn't romance in the Bible? The Song of Songs is a wonderful book for a young couple to read. It is a very sensuous book!

When "Been There, Done That" Is a Bad Thing

Sex is everywhere we look. In a society saturated by sex and sexuality, and a culture whose values are radically different than God's values, many Christian men and women have had sex outside of marriage. Sometimes these encounters occurred before they became a Christian, sometimes not.

The Bible is explicit in stating that the only time sexual intercourse is okay is in marriage, between a husband and his wife. Any other sexual coupling is sinful and can yield negative consequences in your lifetime and eternally. Pre-marital or post-marital sex, extra-marital sex (adultery), and any other manner of sexual intercourse and involvement are sin.

Nonconsensual sex within marriage is a sin; it is rape or sexual assault whether your spouse is awake, passed out, or asleep. Spouses can be charged with a crime. The Lord's way is for consensual, mutually desired sex within marriage, period.

The good news is that sin is forgivable when confessed and turned away from. If you've been involved in any kind of sinful sexual relation, talk with your pastor or a Christian therapist and unload the baggage. Don't carry it into a new marriage. If you already have, or if it's something you've gotten into since you've been married, you've got work to do and you may need to include your spouse.

Leave the Past Behind

One of the consequences of sex outside of marriage (as well as divorce and remarriage) is comparison. When the ghosts of relationships past come into the bedroom, they can wreak havoc if allowed. Your spouse may be both curious to the point of insisting on details and repulsed by your having been with someone else or hearing what you did with them.

For this reason, it's best not to reveal details of former sexual experiences. They are in the past; leave them there. Even if your spouse insists, it will do him or her no good to hear details. Sharing details only gives the ghost more power. In fact, if your spouse was previously married and hurt by the divorce or prior relationships, forcing them to give up details about that sexual experience can be cruel.

Don't ever force or try to guilt your spouse into telling you about a past relationship. Whatever needed to be said should have been said in pre-marital counseling. If it wasn't, then get some counseling now and let a therapist help you deal with prior relationships in a healthy and appropriate manner. In the meantime, focus on the fact that your relationship now is the most important relationship for you both. Focus on the present and the future and let things be new again.

What Should Be Disclosed?

As much as the two of you don't need past sexual encounters to encumber your marriage, if it was very important for you to know your spouse's sexual history you needed to get it before marriage. If there are indications of sexually deviant behavior, you may have to get more information so that you can deal with the issues with your intended.

Things that have the potential to hurt the relationship, such as addictions, deviancies, abuse, infidelity, and so forth while in other relationships are valuable pieces of information about a person that can very much influence your decision to enter into marriage.

For Him and Her

If either or both of you have had sexual partners prior to your marriage, see a doctor to get an AIDS test and check for any sign of a sexually transmitted disease (STD). If you have an STD, you must tell your to-be spouse before you marry and take whatever precautions you can to protect them from getting the disease after you are married. You may also need to work through forgiveness and healing from your pre-marital sexual sins with your pastor to exorcise every ghost of old relationships.

Gentleness Is Important in Both Words and Actions

Why make a point about gentleness? Our sexuality cuts through to the deepest part of our being and is closely connected to our soul. This means that in our sexuality resides the most vulnerable part of our being. In our sexuality we can experience the greatest ecstasy and the greatest pain, the highest of highs and the lowest of lows. Our sexuality must be handled with care always and in all ways.

In 1 John 3:18 we are reminded to "stop just saying we love each other; let us really show it by our actions." Love is shown in both words and actions. Gentleness is shown in our attitude, in what we say, in how we say it, and what we actually do.

You can bless your spouse tremendously and hurt your spouse terribly through your sexual expressions with each other. Practicing the fruit of the spirit is essential in working through your sexual relationship.

Word from the Wise

"But when the Holy Spirit controls our lives, he will produce this kind of fruit in us: love, joy, peace, patience, kindness, goodness, faithfulness, gentleness, and self-control." (Galatians 5:22-23)

Allowing the Holy Spirit to penetrate our lives will produce the fruit of the Spirit. The marriage bed can't wait for the fruit to grow in you. You need to live out the fruit of the Spirit whether you feel like it or not!

Because of the potential for deep (and sometimes lasting) pain, there are couples who resign themselves to no sex, occasional sex, duty sex, and the like to avoid dealing with sexual issues. This is very sad and it need not be. We can prevent this by being gentle, open, and honest with each other and seeking help when we are in pain that we can't deal with together.

Sex has the potential to be the biggest blessing or the biggest curse of our marriages. Let it be a blessing. Remember, sex is like a garden, full of goodness, but requiring care.

 For Her

Men typically don't open up easily about sensitive issues. That doesn't mean they never will, but it probably won't happen as quickly as you would like. Avoid pressuring him, but find a gentle way to remind and encourage him. Help him to feel safe just as you want him to help you feel safe in your relationship. Just because a guy puts up a tough exterior does not mean he's tough on the inside. Pushing him to talk before he's ready will only make it harder to get him to talk again.

Be Patient, Be Kind, Be Real, Be Loose

First Corinthians 13:4-7 is the heart of what's known as the Love Chapter of the Bible. In a mere 65 words, Paul provides what amounts to a formula for a successful marriage. He writes:

> "Love is patient and kind. Love is not jealous or boastful or proud or rude. Love does not demand its own way. Love is not irritable, and it keeps no record of when it has been wronged. It is never glad about injustice but rejoices whenever the truth wins out. Love never gives up, never loses faith, is always hopeful, and endures through every circumstance."

We all desire to be loved in the way Paul describes. We want others to extend us endless patience and kindness. We want to be believed in all the time. We want someone special to always think the best of us, to be happy or sad with us, and to give us our own space while being very close—all at the same time!

That's what we want. But is it what we give? Probably not all of the time. But still our goal should be to apply these guidelines as often as possible to every area of our married life, especially in the bedroom.

It is in the act of sex that we are often the most vulnerable and the most human. It can be too easy to be selfish, inconsiderate, hurried, or distracted while making love. It's easy to inadvertently do or say something that can hurt, offend, or embarrass the other. Why is it so easy? Because we are human and our sinfulness dogs us even in bed.

For Him and Her

Want to stop an endless argument? Make a pact with your spouse to do the following: At any time during an argument, if one of you says, "Let's take it to the closet," then you both immediately go to your bedroom, take off your clothes, get in your closet, hold hands, and try to continue the argument. You just may discover that whatever you were arguing about really isn't all that important anyway.

So what should we do to help? Read those 65 words every day prayerfully. As you read them, reaffirm in your heart your commitment to your spouse. If you have been demanding or irritable, confess these to the Lord and ask his forgiveness. Do the same thing with your spouse. Throughout your day, think of ways that you can be more supportive and encouraging to your spouse. And as any offense they may have caused you comes to mind, forgive it and let it go, and be ready to accept any responsibility you may have for causing them offense. You may even want to read these verses together with your spouse just before you make love.

As you journey together, in and out of bed, joyfully be yourself and accept your spouse just as they are. Allow each other room to mess up and try again. Learn how to laugh at yourself. Before picking at your beloved's "faults" be sure you have closely examined your own life, with the help of the Holy Spirit. And once an issue is settled, leave it settled. When you forgive, mean it.

Dr. Truth

Men—show your wife romance and passion, as well as diligently working to provide an income and keeping the home safe (repaired, etc.). Honor her above all others. Women—show your husband respect and treat him with dignity, especially in front of your children and others. Acknowledge his accomplishments and point them out to others.

Love and trust are choices. Even if your spouse has done something that was hurtful or betrayed your trust, the situation is not irreconcilable. Where Christ is, there is always hope! Reconciliation and healing are always possible, but you have to choose them. When your spouse apologizes and asks forgiveness, no matter how small or big the offense, allow the Holy Spirit to renew the intimacy of your hearts.

Chapter 4

Another Time Married

Getting married again after divorce or the death of a spouse is a blessing with challenges. It's so easy to look at your new spouse and compare him or her to your former spouse.

If the previous relationship was marred by dysfunction, infidelity, abuse, or any other woundings, it's all too easy to expect a repeat in the new relationship. It's one thing to be on guard; it's another to "see" things that aren't really there.

This marriage is not the same as the last one. You have before you a different person and new opportunities. You can rewrite marriage. You can rewrite your sex life. You are free to talk with your new spouse about all of the intimate things you may have wanted to do or try but just couldn't with your former spouse. The opportunities, the adventure, are endless!

The Past Does Not Predict the Future

It is often generally accepted that a reliable predictor of future behavior is past behavior. While there is truth to this, it is not an absolute. It is our best guess of the future if there has been no intervention, no counseling, no personal challenging of old things, no willingness, desire or effort to change.

If you are in a new relationship because the first one ended in divorce, you've probably done some soul searching and, hopefully, gotten some counseling. Coming from a relationship that was not working ought to have encouraged you to seek help to understand what happened in that relationship and who you were in that relationship. There are two things that play into any relationship's going sour: one is our personal self and the other is who we were in relation to the person we married. While our spouse doesn't cause our behavior, we make decisions about how we react to that person. Your reactions may have been as unhealthy as the other person's behaviors.

Considering that the pain of divorce runs deep and raises many personal issues, we presume that you have taken steps to deal with yourself and gain insight into your personality. We also presume that you have considered any family of origin issues and that you have either made efforts to heal from past issues or that you are doing so now. If you haven't, consider that you may have some personal work to do so that you don't bring old relationship issues into a new relationship.

Think of marriage as a dance. Have you seen really good dancers on a dance floor? Those who make it look effortless and beautiful? This is how you want your new relationship to be. People who divorce weren't dancing well together. The way that you and your former spouse related to each other fell into a pattern. The pattern didn't work. Your new spouse does not dance the same way as your former spouse; you don't have those same patterns anymore. You and your new spouse will naturally develop your own dance. Your reading this book is like taking dancing lessons. You want new, healthy, rewarding patterns to form.

Word from the Wise

"Get rid of all bitterness, rage, anger, harsh words, and slander, as well as all types of malicious behavior. Instead, be kind to each other, tenderhearted, forgiving one another, just as God through Christ has forgiven you." (Ephesians 4:31-32)

Because of our faith in Jesus Christ, because of what the Spirit of God can do in us when we invite him, we can truly transform ourselves and be transformed.

Your New Relationship

If you are in a new relationship because the first one ended in the death of your spouse, you will also have done some soul searching. Perhaps you have grieved because you were madly in love and had a good marriage. If you had a painful marriage, it's possible that you felt a sense of relief when your spouse died. In this case you probably have feelings similar to those of a divorced person.

If you had a good marriage that ended, you most likely won't be concerned about the past predicting the future. If the past was good, you'll be making the same presumption about the future. If you were in a good marriage where there was lots of love, consideration, understanding, and good sex, it's most likely that you will find another relationship that is as healthy as the last.

But you will still be married to a different person. Your risk will be to unfairly expect your new spouse to do the things your old spouse did. Presuming that your spouse will or should or ought to do what the previous one did is a mistake that can be toxic to the marriage. Your new spouse can easily fall into thinking that they won't measure up to your former spouse or that they are always being compared. Resist the urge to predict your spouse's behaviors based on those of your former spouse.

There will be things that your new spouse does that will remind you of your former spouse. You can fall into two sins: you may react the way you did with your former spouse or you may presume that your new spouse has the same intentions as your former spouse. You may have to work hard to remind yourself that this isn't the "ex" in front of you, this is a new person, who loves you and is committed to you and wants to have a good life with you. He or she doesn't want to be involved in unhealthy patterns. You, too, are a new person with new choices and options as to how you will react to your new spouse.

For example, the wife says to her new husband, "Sweetheart, would you please take out the trash?" The new husband says, "Sure, soon as the news is over." The wife becomes angry because her husband isn't doing it *right now*. But after the news, her husband gets up and takes out the trash.

The wife became angry because she assumed that her new husband's "soon as the news is over" statement meant he wasn't going to do it at all. In her previous marriage her husband let the trash build up on the porch, no matter how many requests or reminders from her. Her temptation was to judge him prematurely based on her experiences with the "ex." The challenge was to restrain herself and wait to see what her husband did. If she let her anger cause her to pressure him to take out the trash "right now," she would be starting a fight for no reason. Her new husband was more responsible and receptive than her previous husband, but at the beginning of the marriage she will only be finding this out.

Focusing on the Newness

As a Christian you know of the transforming power of the Holy Spirit; you know that you can put off the old self and take on a new self. Before you accepted Christ as your Lord and Savior, your behavior was sure to be sinful. After becoming a Christian, the old behaviors began to fade. Change is possible. Armed with your past experience and the growth that came as a result, you have chosen to enter a new relationship. Sure, some elements of your new marriage will be similar to your previous one. But it's important to keep in mind that it's not the same marriage and that you are not necessarily fated to commit or be subjected to the same mistakes.

It also means you have a new partner in the bedroom. You will need to relearn how to make love since your new spouse will have different likes and dislikes. The same holds true for them. They need to learn about you. In this situation, making comparisons can also be damaging to a relationship.

Focus instead on the newness. Become "little children" again and pretend you're learning about sex for the first time. Reclaim a sense of innocence and allow yourself to fully enjoy the uniqueness and freshness of your new spouse.

Word from the Wise

"There must be a spiritual renewal of your thoughts and attitudes. You must display a new nature because you are a new person, created in God's likeness–righteous, holy, and true." (Ephesians 4: 23,24)

Being *in Christ*, you can change and alter both your behaviors and attitudes. Be open to the newness of each other and draw on your Christian faith to challenge you into personal and marital growth.

Keeping Ghosts Out of the Bedroom

Regardless of what has brought you to remarriage, letting go of the past is essential, especially in the bedroom. Few topics can kill the mood faster than bringing up a former husband or wife. That's almost like bringing another person into the bedroom; your spouse will feel like he or she is in a competition.

If you need to talk about your former spouse you shouldn't do it while in bed with your new spouse. Rather, do it in the living room or out at a coffeehouse. Don't let your old spouse into your new bed!

Word from the Wise

"… bringing into captivity every thought to the obedience of Christ." 2 Corinthians 10:5

If you are in bed and are beginning a time of intimacy with your new spouse and you have a thought about your former spouse or a past relationship, snuff it out!

Nothing kills the mood faster than if you choose to share your thought. In fact, this is pure sabotage of intimacy with your new spouse.

Part of our healing from the old is talking about what has happened in the past and working and grieving through it. Your new spouse may be a wonderful person to help you do this—or not. Issues you may have had with your former spouse may be too much for your new spouse to deal with; perhaps you will have to consider speaking with a therapist alone to deal with your issues. Your pastor or spiritual accountability partner could help with the spiritual dimension. This doesn't mean that your new spouse doesn't love you. It just means they recognize their personal, human limitations, that's all.

For Her

Your former spouse may have done some unusual things sexually or personally that made you feel uncomfortable. You may think that your new spouse will be able to handle listening to the details. However, he may find these things too offensive or painful to hear and may not want his mind contaminated with these images. Take your stories to your pastor or counselor if you have to get them off your chest.

It doesn't matter if you have positive or negative things to say about your former spouse and your previous sex life. Even if you want to talk about all the great sexual experiences you had with your former spouse, don't! Your new spouse may begin to feel that he or she could never measure up to your expectations. Your new spouse may ask you why you didn't stay married to the previous spouse if he or she was "that good." Even if your previous spouse passed away, your new spouse will feel like he or she is playing second fiddle and will never be good enough for you.

For Him

Look at her, your beauty, your love! She is a completely unique and wonderful creation of God. Discover who she is! Look for her uniqueness. Give thanks to God for her every day. Commit yourself to making this a good marriage, a great marriage, a new marriage.

If you think about something that was great about sex with your former spouse, share it in careful language. You don't have to mention the spouse, just the type of thing they did that brought you pleasure. Watch your language.

Instead of: "When George used to lick my ear with his tongue I used to get really turned on."

Try: "I find it really stimulating to feel a wet tongue in my ear. It's a turn-on for me."

See the difference?

Your references to your former spouse may be subtle. Check with your spouse to find out if you are making them uncomfortable with what you say about your former spouse and your sex life together.

Taking Hold of New Things: The New Person Is a Different Person

How can you let go of the past? Take hold of the new person lying there beside you in bed! Focus your attention on your spouse and his or her unique qualities.

For Her

This is the man you have chosen to love and commit your life to. He is a unique individual. You don't know all of his thoughts, desires, or preferences yet. How will you discover what they are? Every aspect of marriage involves an investment. Invest in him. Discover him.

What do you love the most about your new husband? What color are his eyes? What excites him in and out of bed? What were the qualities that originally drew you to her? What's her favorite scent and where does she wear it? Invest the same time and energy in getting to know them as you did in getting to know your previous spouse.

When it comes to sex, you'll both need to talk about your likes and dislikes in the bedroom. You may discover that something your former spouse was very turned on by is uncomfortable and embarrassing to your new spouse. If that's the case, don't force the issue or try to guilt them into going along. Be respectful and loving and work together to develop your own, new, special repertoire of sexual play and turn-ons.

Dr. Truth

> You have entered a new marriage, you have begun a new life. This part of life will be better than what came before. It will be better because you and your spouse are taking responsibility for making it better. As you invest in your marriage, in each other and in a good sex life, it will become the relationship that you always wished you had.

What You Wanted and More!

You're in a brand new marriage with a brand new person. All the mistakes you may have made in your former marriage are, in a sense, erased. It's time for a fresh start and you've been blessed with a new mate who's just right for you—and for whom you are just right. Let the fun begin!

You're more experienced in life and wiser. You are better equipped to be a great husband or wife. You've overcome your fumbling and shyness in the bedroom. Life is good and the sex can be fantastic.

Instead of nervousness and fear, you can now enter into this new marriage with confidence, knowledge, and wisdom—all elements of good sex! Enjoy that man of yours to the fullest. Embrace that vision of your woman every chance you get. Enjoy the new, fresh experiences that are yours to partake in.

Husbands, surprise your new wife with a weekend at a nearby resort hotel. Get a room with a private Jacuzzi, for two. Book a massage for two. Buy her a nice silk nightie with matching robe and get yourself a pair of silk PJ's. Then stay in your room and have a great time.

Wives, get tickets to the big football game and go with your husband. After the game, tell him you've got reservations at a nearby hotel. Have room service bring up his favorite meal and then tell him you have a few plays and moves you'd like to show him—in bed.

Whatever it is that you've always wanted to do or try, now is your second chance. Go for it!

 For Him and Her

> Hey, you don't have to go too far from home to start something new with your life. Book the kids to be with their friends for a night, run her a hot bath, get some massage oil, set up a room full of candles, light them when she's in the tub, put on some soft music, scrub her back, slip into the tub with her ... (your imagination can do the rest).

Chapter 5

Some Preliminary Considerations

An old song declared, "Love and marriage go together like a horse and carriage." What the heck does that mean? Maybe it means that men and women are different and that, while there are obvious challenges to be overcome, it is possible for a man and woman to cooperate in a mutually satisfying relationship.

Health and Sex: Nausea and Sex Make a Volatile Combination

We don't have sex in a vacuum. Humans can't have sex outside the context of who they are and what is happening to themselves, their spouse, and their loved ones.

Our overall health involves our physical, emotional, and spiritual health. Problems in any of these can cause us to have to suspend or shift our sexual hopes, dreams, and expectations. When we are not well in any of those areas our interest in sex can diminish or disappear.

Physical Considerations

Medications can interfere with sexual functioning. If you are experiencing sexual difficulties (inability to get or sustain an erection, inability to have orgasm) and you are on medications, check your information sheet and see if there are "sexual side effects" listed. If there aren't you can do an Internet search on the medication, which may give you more information than the information sheet you received with your prescription. You can also call your pharmacist and ask them directly. If there is any possibility that your sexual problems could be related to the medications you are on, talk with your doctor about it. There may be another medication available that treats your condition without sexual side effects.

Major depression, a medical condition, can hamper your sex life and so can some of the anti-depressant medications to treat it. High blood pressure medications can affect sexual performance as can cholesterol-lowering drugs. Again, check with your doctor if you are concerned.

There are physical conditions that affect sex as well. The most obvious is impotence, but there is also vaginismus, venereal disease, and prostate problems. Bladder infections, gastro-intestinal disorders, acid reflux, diverticulitis, and hemorrhoids can make sex uncomfortable and difficult.

Pregnancy, hemorrhoids, vaginal infections, vertigo, nausea—many physical conditions can also affect our sexual interests or physical abilities. Who feels like having sex when they could run to the toilet any minute with vomiting or diarrhea? Who feels like having sex when they are so depressed they can't even get up in the morning? When our bodies are not healthy, sex may be the last thing on our minds.

Be aware that some people still want sexual intimacy as a comfort during illness. It may be difficult for the healthy spouse to consider making love under such conditions. It puts the sick person in a vulnerable position to ask for sex; they are already vulnerable and are opening themselves up to rejection. Try to consider what your sick spouse needs and be open to it. On the other hand, if the healthy spouse wants sex with the sick spouse, it may be difficult for the sick spouse to consider his or her needs when they are barely surviving their own. Sex while you're physically sick is a very sensitive issue for both spouses, and should be resolved as a couple.

Emotional Considerations

When some people are emotionally upset or stressed they want more sex; others want less or none. Emotional stress can cause our sex drive to go either way.

As mentioned above, major depression has an effect on our entire body, not just our emotions. Depression can cause a drop in sexual drive and interest. If your spouse becomes depressed you will want to talk with them about their feelings about sexual involvement. They may respond to your interest in sex as loving or offensive. It could go either way. There is no way to know until you bring up the issue.

If one of you loses your job, you may be too emotionally distressed to have any energy or focus for sex. On the other hand, sex could bring you some comfort amidst your pain.

Women's hormones are a blessing and a curse (of sorts). That PMS stuff can bring agitation, irritation, anger, mood swings, and complete disinterest in sex. Just before a woman ovulates her hormones are inviting sex (her body wants to get pregnant) so she'll be more sexually excitable, lubricated and, usually, mellow. That extra dose of estrogen is a good thing for sex.

All this to say, our emotions and our hormones can affect our interest in sex. They are just one more thing to consider in the mix.

Spiritual Considerations

As much as people can be affected by medical and emotional conditions, we can also be affected by our spiritual condition.

Sometimes in our walk with the Lord we come to a desert. We feel lost and alone spiritually. We struggle with what the Lord is telling us or the fact that we don't feel that we're hearing him. When our spirit and our minds are distracted with spiritual issues, our bodies and their needs take second place. We may neither have the energy or interest in sexual things when we are preoccupied with spiritual things.

Sometimes we devote our minds, hearts, and souls to greater pursuit of intimacy with God. This is the time when Paul says it's okay to refrain from sexual intercourse.

Word from the Wise

"So do not deprive each other of sexual relations. The only exception to this rule would be the agreement of both husband and wife to refrain from sexual intimacy for a limited time, so they can give themselves more completely to prayer. Afterward they should come together again so that Satan won't be able to tempt them because of their lack of self-control." (1 Corinthians 7:5-6)

This time of refraining from intimacy has two requirements: that the couple be in agreement and that the time be limited.

On the other hand, when our spirits are one with the Father, the Son, and the Holy Spirit, when we sense that we are in the hand of God and walking on just the path he wants us on, we feel so much more personal freedom and our bodies can be much more sensitized to sexual feelings. Sexual union with our spouses at these times offers a pinnacle of delight like no other. We are aware of intimacy with the Godhead and the ecstasy of it. It is not surprising that human ecstasy with our spouses would become part of our overall appreciation of our Father and what he has given us—sexual unity with our spouse.

Age and Sex: It's Not the Wrinkles That Slow Things Down

The older you get, the better you get at sex. Young people don't know the first thing about sex. We all start off with no knowledge and no experience. As we get older we gain knowledge and experience. Good sex is something you learn along the way both through education and personal experiences with your mate.

Younger couples may have more sex more often but older couples can have more sustained and enjoyable sexual interactions. Sex when you are young can be a whole lot of quick encounters and trying new things, some that work, some that don't. Older couples have a familiarity with each other. They have learned how to truly please each other, they take more time for sex and can often get much more pleasure from it than the young.

Time and time again studies show a correlation between an active sex life and longevity. Of course, no one knows if longevity and good health make a good sex life possible or if a good sex life brings good health and longevity. It is probably safe to say that those who are having sex in their elder years are people who are getting along well with one another and are basically contented with their married life. They are probably people at peace in more ways than one. When you're at peace, sex is a sheer pleasure and you want it.

Things that inhibit us when we get older have to do with physical limitations on account of disability or illness, not on the physiological capacity of our aging bodies to be able to experience sexual pleasure.

Gender and Sex: Differences Can Be Confusing

In training to become a psychologist or marriage counselor in the 80's we were taught that differences between the sexes were few and far between.

The unalterable truth is: Men and women are wired differently. They think differently, their physiology is different, their hormones are different, their emotions work differently, they communicate differently.

Linguistics professor and author Deborah Tannen has spent a lifetime studying the variations in communication and interactions among men and women. In one study, she used a room in which there were two chairs. Pairs of males and pairs of females, from children to adults, were told to go into the room and talk. Consistently, the females would go into the room and position the chairs so that they were facing each other as they talked more or less as equals. With each pair of males, one would take what Tannen calls the "one up" role while the other fell into the "one down" role. The "one up" male would position the chairs side by side so that as they talked, they seldom made eye contact.

Despite these differences, experts agree that one way to a great sex life comes through effective communication. Women say, "Hooray!" Men say, "Oh, no!" Of course these are generalizations. Roughly 8 or 9 out of 10 men are uncomfortable talking with their wife about sex. About half of all women are uncomfortable talking with their husbands about sex. What's the problem? Fear.

Men often are afraid they won't be able to please their wives. They tend to believe they should naturally be able to give their wives total satisfaction. If a wife wants to talk about sex, doesn't that mean the husband is doing something wrong? This makes the husband feel that he's somehow a failure. He gets defensive or wants to avoid the conversation. It takes a lot for most men to sit down and have a conversation about sex.

One husband, from the beginning of the marriage, had problems maintaining an erection yet experienced nocturnal emissions. This situation indicated that his potency was emotionally constrained. Counseling revealed that he didn't have a clue what to do with his wife sexually and was terrified that he would never be able to satisfy her. He couldn't talk about this and his fear led to his impotence. Once he began to express his fears and was helped to talk openly with his wife, he became able to achieve erections and please his wife.

Many women are reluctant to talk about sex as well. The reluctant woman may be terribly shy, easily embarrassed, introverted, or have had negative sexual experiences leaving her uptight about her body and uncomfortable with her husband's body.

Regardless of your comfort level on the topic of sex, it's okay! If you are hesitant, you can learn, over time, to open up little by little. If you're eager to talk, you may need to restrain yourself if your mate isn't. Be patient with each other and don't give up if initial discussions don't go as smoothly as you would like.

For Her

Many women say to each other something like "Men, are they dumb or just plain stupid? They just don't get it. Will they ever understand us?" No, men don't understand us totally. They will never truly understand what makes us tick. But you've married a loving man who is willing to try and make his best effort to "get it." As much as he is reluctant, you must be persistent and willing to put up with a certain amount of his frustration, anger, confusion, and embarrassment to be understood. Keep your cool and speak from your heart.

Having a conversation with each other won't be unlike a lot of your other conversations about any delicate issue. Remember, sex is always a delicate issue because it is part of the core of our self, right next to our soul. Most people will be able to talk about their sex life at home, alone. Some couples can't do this because one or both of the spouses just can't talk about sex, period. These couples need a third party, trained and qualified to help them work through their sexual issues.

If you are unhappy with your sex life and your spouse refuses to talk, you should push, pull, or drag him or her with you to a counselor. Make sure this counselor is coming from a Christian worldview, or at least know where he or she deviates and discount that part of the guidance. If he or she won't go, then go alone and learn what you can do to help open things up between you. A good therapist can equip you with practical tools for encouraging your reluctant spouse to feel safe about talking about sex. Again, be patient and loving.

For Him

When women are PMSing they are more emotional, and when they are more emotional they want to talk about all of the "issues." If you want to avoid an overly emotional discussion about sex, talk with her about her cycle and pick a time when she most likely won't be as emotional. Then, encourage her to talk about the things that concern her.

When men listen to women talk with each other they are often stunned that they are so willing to share deep personal things, talk so fast, and get so energized. When women listen to men talk they wonder how they can understand each other, why they didn't finish talking about the topic they started on, and whether they communicated at all.

For example, when women talk they will share infinite detail. If they are old friends or just met, by the end of the conversation they will know the names, ages, grades, hopes, and dreams of each other, each others' children, each others' spouses, how their homes are decorated, what their favorite foods and colors are, the last ten books they've read, and the movie that makes them cry.

On the other hand, two men can spend an entire day or weekend together, and upon their return home not be able to answer any question posed by their wives related to any of the information listed above. When asked, "So what did you talk about the whole time?" the reply will be, "I don't know, sports and guy stuff I guess."

The point is, men and women are different creatures, in the bedroom and out. We have a gender gap to cross when it comes to communicating about sex, and everything else.

Putting It All Together

So with all this stuff going on, how can a couple expect to be satisfied in bed and successful as a couple? Well, it's a mystery—a great mystery! Take a look at what Paul says:

> "And further, you will submit to one another out of reverence for Christ. You wives will submit to your husbands as you do to the Lord. For a husband is the head of his wife as Christ is the head of his body, the church; he gave his life to be her Savior. As the church submits to Christ, so you wives must submit to your husbands in everything. And you husbands must love your wives with the same love Christ showed the church. He gave up his life for her to make her holy and clean, washed by baptism and God's word. He did this to present her to himself as a glorious church without a spot or wrinkle or any other blemish. Instead, she will be holy and without fault. In the same way, husbands ought to love their wives as they love their own bodies. For a man is actually loving himself when he loves his wife. No one hates his own body but lovingly cares for it, just as Christ cares for his body, which is the church. And we are his body. As the scriptures say, 'A man leaves his father and mother and is joined to his wife, and the two are united into one.' This is a great mystery, but it is an illustration of the way Christ and the

church are one. So again I say, each man must love his wife as he loves himself, and the wife must respect her husband. (Ephesians 5:21-33)"

Without getting into a detailed analysis of the scripture (which could fill volumes), let's summarize the essentials in five main points:

- Reverent submission: Submission is a loaded term for some, but it need not be, especially when coupled with reverence. It means to humbly revere one another equally. This cannot be demanded of only one; it is a requirement of husband and wife toward each other in a Christ-like manner. It grows out of your personal submission to the will and love of Jesus Christ and is enabled through the power of the Holy Spirit.

- Beneficent selflessness: Are you willing to die for your spouse? There will be opportunities every day! This means more than giving up your physical life for another, although that's included. It means that both will need to lay down (sacrifice) aspects of their pre-marital lives to remove barriers of intimacy within the marriage. It can be as simple as giving up always eating dinner in front of the TV to something as profound as giving up a country and culture.

- Mutual holiness: Few marriages fail when true spirituality is alive in each partner. The goal is to "be holy and without fault," which can only come through a consistent walk in Christ. Praying together, having devotions together, attending and being involved in church together, can all contribute to a strong marital faith. Each must also carefully and faithfully nurture their personal relationship with God.

Word from the Wise

"In the same way, you husbands must give honor to your wives. Treat her with understanding as you live together. She may be weaker than you are, but she is your equal partner in God's gift of new life. If you don't treat her as you should, your prayers will not be heard." (1 Peter 3:7)

This means lovingly providing godly leadership with a servant heart, and with gentleness and respect. But a man who exhibits dominating tendencies offends God, hurts his wife, and will have his prayers ignored.

- Complete commitment: Once married there is no other more important earthly relationship. Family members, friends, relatives, and acquaintances need to hold a far lesser place in your priorities than your spouse. Any time another relationship becomes a source of tension in a marriage, if the issue causing the tension cannot be reconciled, the relationship may need to be severed or at least distanced.

- Loving respect: You each bring talent, wisdom, experiences, knowledge, and more to the relationship. While what you each bring may be different it is no less valuable. It's probably those differences that created a good deal of the initial attraction to one another. God has drawn you together to complement one another, not be mirror reflections! Learn to admire and cherish the differences in your mate. Pray that God allows you to see your spouse the way he sees them and to also understand all the ways you both fit together.

Nearly every aspect of marriage, including sex, will present challenges to you as a couple and as individuals. Some days will go well, many days something will go wrong. Keeping your marriage vital requires effort that will pay off in great sex, among other things. Above all, invite the Holy Spirit into your daily routine, and even into your conflicts. When you are unable to see a solution to a problem, God can clear it all up for you. Keep the five points above in mind daily and you'll both do well.

Part 2

The Fun Part

Now that we've taken care of some of the preliminaries, it's time to get down to it! Well, almost. Knowing about your body and your spouse's body will help improve your sex life in marriage. For both of you, there are some cautions to consider as far as being gentle in certain areas. And there are other parts that need a lot of attention.

Beyond the body parts, however, great sex happens when the whole person is actively engaged. Take time to take care of each other before and after making love, and watch those fireworks happen while making love!

Chapter 6

How Her Body Works

Great sex requires an understanding of your body parts as well as those of your spouse.

What Girls Learned in Grade School

Do you remember what they taught you in grade school in the "sex" class?

Let's see, they told you about your fallopian tubes, your ovaries, your womb, and your pituitary gland. You learned that the pituitary gland is responsible for the onset of menstruation, breast development, and secondary hair growth (pubic and underarm hair). You learned about your menstrual cycle and how babies are made. You may also have been taught about hygiene and controlling your greasy hair, pimply face, and body odor.

Depending on how comfortable your teacher was, you got more or less information. Did anyone feel comfortable enough to ask a question?

Did anybody teach you that God created your body in a unique and particular way for sexual pleasure, not just reproduction? Did anyone tell you that females can have a female version of the "wet dream?"

While you need to start with the basics we will go far beyond the basics so that you fully come to know how much work God put into you so that you could enjoy what he made. For you to understand the pleasure of your body, you really don't need to get into reproduction and all the technical medical stuff. You can get that basic medical information many places. In this book you will learn only as much as is necessary to understand what contributes to the wonder of your body in sexual pleasure and lovemaking.

 Word from the Wise

"Thank you for making me so wonderfully complex! Your workmanship is marvelous—and how well I know it. You watched me as I was being formed in utter seclusion, as I was woven together in the dark of the womb." (Psalm 139:14-15)

Our Heavenly Father made us perfect in his sight. He handcrafted every intimate part of our being. The beauty of our bodies and the wonders of sexual passion and pleasure were given intentional thought by God.

The Parts and What They Do

How do you get sexual pleasure? You get sexual pleasure from many body parts. You have what you might call primary and secondary sexually pleasurable parts.

The primary sexual response organs are the organs that produce the pleasurable pulsating, contracting sensations involved directly in orgasm: the clitoris, the labia minora, and the vaginal tissues closest to the labia minora.

The secondary sexual response organs include the breasts, mouth, lips, and skin.

Every woman is a little different and will tell you that stimulating her here or there works best for her. Women need to pay attention to their responses to being touched in different ways on different parts of her body, being sure to let their husbands know what works for her. If you don't know what works for you, it's time to learn.

For Her

Talk to your man. It's a mistake to think that your husband knows what makes you tick sexually. Only you know exactly what brings you pleasure and what doesn't. How is he going to find out unless you tell him? Yep, you need to tell him, whether he asks or not, whether he is comfortable with the conversation or not! You'll find that even if he's uncomfortable, he'll pay attention to what you say and start doing those very things.

The Clitoris

Did you know that when God created the clitoris in women he had women's sexual pleasure in mind? Unlike your husband's penis, which has two purposes (urination and ejaculation), the clitoris has one function: sexual pleasure. It serves no other function in a woman's body. The clitoris is to the woman as the head of the penis is to the man—both have the highest concentration of sensitive nerve endings that respond with sexual pleasure to stimulation.

The clitoris is the pivotal center of orgasm for the woman. Many parts of a woman produce and enhance sexual stimulation but orgasm bursts forth from the clitoris (although many women would argue that stimulation of the labia minora and the vaginal tissue next to it are equal to the clitoris in this department).

Most women know little about their clitoris. If you haven't seen yours, you should take a look. You'll need a hand mirror and perhaps a flashlight. Don't be shocked. It's your body. You should know where your clitoris is and what it looks like.

For Him

If you really want to please your wife you need to do two things: (1) pay attention to what she responds to and (2) ask her what you can do that will give her the greatest pleasure. Sometimes women give up on sex because their husbands keep doing the same thing, the wrong thing, and they feel they will offend their husband by telling him this.

The clitoris has a hood of skin over it (like a man's foreskin) so you'll have to pull it back to actually see what it looks like. Touch it and see what it feels like. The head of the clitoris is a little nodule of cartilage like that found at the tip of your nose. The head is at the end of a shaft. The shaft feels soft and pliable, sort of like your ear lobe. Both the head and the shaft are highly sensitive to stimulation.

Does this feel embarrassing? If you grew up in a home where little information was given about your body and your parents avoided talking about sexual stuff (lest you prematurely do something you weren't supposed to do), you might feel a certain amount of embarrassment at the thought of looking at your own body. Even if your family was more open, for many people, looking at or touching their own bodies is foreign and uncomfortable. It really is okay to take a look at and touch your own parts.

The Labia Minora

The labia majora doesn't have many nerve endings and is just a flap of skin with little sensation. Its purpose is to protect the vaginal opening. The labia majora generally flattens during stimulation of other more sensitive areas. It is the labia minora that is full of nerve endings and highly sensitive to touch. Many women can come to orgasm through stimulation of the labia minora and the vagina without any contact with the clitoris. Gentle stroking of this tissue brings wonderful, exciting feelings.

The Vagina

The vagina itself can be over four inches deep. Deep inside the vagina there is very little sensation to touch. It is only the outer part of the vagina that holds a vast number of nerve endings which, when stimulated, can bring pleasurable excitement for a woman. The highly sensitive area goes about an inch into the vaginal canal.

The Perineum

The perineum is skin between the anus and the vaginal opening. Many women report that touch to this area is also highly erogenous.

The Breasts

There are women who say that attention to their breasts holds the greatest stimulation. Stimulation can come from caressing the entire breast with the hand, and from licking and sucking and from pinching the nipple. Because the sensations in the breast can change during lovemaking, there are times when pinching hurts and times when pinching adds to the pleasure. Also, depending on where a woman is in her menstrual cycle, her breasts are more or less sensitive and touching them may bring pain and discomfort.

The Lips and Mouth

Some people become highly aroused by kissing and licking around the mouth. There are women who can reach orgasm through kissing alone. The mouth and lips also have tons of nerve endings to sense touch and stimulation.

The Skin

The skin is an erogenous organ. It shouldn't be underestimated in lovemaking. Arousal can come from nearly anywhere on the body. Some people become completely aroused by having their ears sucked and licked and feeling their spouse's tongue in their ear. Some women's arousal is increased when they are touched just above their pubic hair while being pleasured in the clitoral/vaginal areas. For some women, touch to the insides or backs of their thighs is highly erogenous. Inner arms, armpits, neck, small of the back, under the foot—the point is, God created us to respond to touch.

Taking Care of the Parts

Since your whole body can receive stimulation in lovemaking, you need to take care of yourself—all of yourself.

Soap and Water

Wash your skin gently. Use mild soaps. Pat dry gently. Be kind when you shave. Moisturize your skin when it's too dry.

When washing your vaginal area, soap gently through all of the external tissues and rinse well so that soap doesn't irritate your sensitive skin. If you have had any pain during intercourse, pull back the hood of skin over the clitoris and gently clean under there with a Q-tip. Sometimes little particles can get caught in there and you may not discover it until you're in the middle of passion. If you've got particles, you've got pain.

Don't douche unless your doctor gives you specific instructions. Douching can increase your risk of vaginal yeast infections because you upset the natural balance of bacteria and yeast in the vagina.

Smells

Many people report that natural body smells coming from a clean body are arousing during lovemaking. Just one look at the animal kingdom tells us plainly that when God created them male and female he gave us two things: (1) sex drive to seek out the other and (2) smells to provide navigation. Our natural smells are part of the way God created us as male and female.

Body sprays, including vaginal sprays, can irritate your skin and irritate your husband. Spraying to mask the scent of unpleasant body odor actually makes the smell worse. If you're stinky or sticky, take a quick shower before lovemaking rather than using scented sprays. Also, using feminine hygiene sprays can put you

 For Him and Her

Keep your toenails trimmed! It puts a damper on lovemaking when one of you lets out a yelp from getting jabbed by a big toe nail.

at greater risk for a vaginal yeast infection because they can upset the natural balance of organisms in the vagina. Don't use deodorized tampons or scented toilet paper for the same reason.

> ### Word from the Wise
>
> "My lover tried to unlatch the door, and my heart thrilled within me. I jumped up to open it. My hands dripped with perfume, my fingers with lovely myrrh, as I pulled back the bolt." Songs of Songs 5:4,5
>
> There is a place for sensual scents, even in the Bible. Just be careful not to indulge in too much of a good thing and be careful where you apply them.

Another Argument for Hygiene: Infections

Women are susceptible to various infections that will affect their love life. Two infections that are usually preventable with proper hygiene are yeast infections and urethra/bladder infections.

Yeast Infections

Yeast infections are messy and itchy. You feel like you want to just rake your vagina because it gets so itchy. When you have a yeast infection you get a yucky, frothy, curdled discharge. Basically a yeast infection occurs when the normal balance of "vaginal flora" is upset inside the vagina (the balance of bacteria and naturally occurring yeast). The bacteria in the vagina keep control of the yeast.

Yeast is an opportunist that will grow wherever conditions are right, namely with regard to pH, moisture, glucose (sugar), competing organisms, and immune response.

Conditions that can increase your chance of a yeast infection include taking birth control pills and antibiotics, having diabetes or being overweight, and prolonged sweating as might occur if wearing tight garments or sitting for long periods of time (such as when you're traveling).

If you weren't taught as a young girl to wipe your bottom front to back you'd better start doing it now. The reason is, urine is sterile and can't hurt your vagina or your anus but feces hurt both your vagina and your urethra (which connects to your bladder).

Feces in the vagina can cause an imbalance of the vaginal environment. The best way to prevent fecal contamination of the vagina and urethra is to wash with soap and water after every bowel movement, but this, of course, isn't always possible. Even using a Tucks pad, wetted toilet paper, or the like to wipe the rectum after a bowel movement is better than just wiping with dry toilet paper. Try to remove all fecal particles with wiping. When you bathe make sure you soap your anus and vaginal tissues well to remove all fecal matter.

It is amazing how many women on antibiotics discover that they have developed a yeast infection. The problem: sugar and antibiotics for women don't mix. When a woman is on antibiotics the "vaginal flora" in her vagina get thrown slightly off balance. There is natural yeast in a woman's vagina, which doesn't cause any trouble. The problems start when the antibiotics kill the bacteria in the vagina that are keeping the yeast under control. Without the normal bacteria there is an imbalance in the yeast. Antibiotics suppress the vagina's ability to control yeast. This isn't a problem as long as the yeast doesn't grow while on the antibiotics.

What causes yeast to grow? Sugar. It's just like baking bread. The yeast won't grow, the bread won't rise, unless there is sugar for the yeast to feed on. When yeast feeds on sugar it produces gas bubbles and makes a stink. When women have a yeast infection they get a frothy discharge that is sometimes stinky. This is because the yeast is getting fed and the vagina isn't able to deal with it.

The moral of the story is: When on antibiotics avoid sugar like the plague (no candy, chocolate bars, desserts, etc.)!

Eating yogurt and acidophilus milk helps the vaginal organisms keep a healthy balance. Wear cotton panties, as they allow the vagina to breathe well. Avoid tight panties, swimwear, workout clothes, leggings, tight fitting pants, and so on. These tight garments stop the air circulating around the vagina and you become more susceptible to yeast infections. If you must buy panties made of synthetic materials, try to make sure they have a cotton crotch.

There are many other things that can make a woman more vulnerable to yeast infections that are not covered here in detail, but you should be aware of them: diabetics with blood sugar out of control, those with autoimmune disorders, people on corticosteroids, being pregnant, overweight, and keeping the vaginal area in too much moisture too long—e.g., staying in water or a wet swimsuit too long.

Urethra/Bladder Infections

If feces particles get into your urethra it can cause infection in the urethra itself which can spread right up into the bladder. Bladder infections are very painful and make intercourse painful too.

Another cause of problems in the urethra is insufficient lubrication of tissues before lovemaking (the drier the tissues are, the greater chance of damage). The urethra can also be damaged by good vigorous lovemaking, especially when the wife is on top of her husband.

When the urethra is torn or bruised inside, a little bit of blood goes into the urine. Because of the damage, bacteria can get inside and begin to grow. This is how the infection starts.

For Her

Did you know that vigorous sex can cause blood in your urine for a day or two? It can and it's not serious. However, if you have to give a urine sample at the doctor's office the next day, you may have some explaining to do! If blood shows up, be sure to tell your doctor why it might be there.

To Pee or Not to Pee, That Is the Question

Women wonder whether they should pee before they make love or afterwards. The advantage of peeing before lovemaking is that you won't be uncomfortable or feel you'll have to get up and go at an awkward time. But the advantages of peeing after lovemaking seriously outweigh the advantage of peeing before.

First of all, women don't need to fear losing their bladder during lovemaking. Once there has been sufficient stimulation the woman's urethra becomes as incapable of releasing urine as a man's penis does when it is erect. If women try to release their bladder too soon after climax, they won't be able to. Only after the muscles around the area have sufficiently relaxed can you release the urine. This takes a couple of minutes.

Second, when the bladder is slightly full it puts a little more pressure on the clitoris, which enhances clitoral stimulation.

The last benefit of urinating after lovemaking is the cleansing of the urethra. Urine is sterile, and if there has been any damage to the urethra during lovemaking and bacteria entered, or if any feces happened to get in there during lovemaking, urinating cleanses the urethra. The fuller the bladder, the better the cleansing. You need to pee as soon after orgasm as possible. If you wait hours, bacteria will already be growing.

The Hirsute Woman: Hair, Hair, Everywhere

Some women are much hairier than others. These are the hirsute women. The hirsute woman is hairier on all parts of her body. The parts of her body where excessive hair can interfere with lovemaking are her breasts and pubic hair.

Some women have very thick, long pubic hairs. Having very long pubic hairs can affect the wife and the husband. As his penis penetrates the vagina, these long hairs can be drawn down into the vagina with the penis and the hairs will pull and hurt her. This can also cause pain for her husband and penetration can be difficult. Either the wife or the husband has to manipulate the hairs to get them out of the way before penetration. Additionally, for the husband to please his wife through clitoral or vaginal stimulation, the hairs can be a hassle to get through. The solution: trim the hairs. There is nothing wrong with trimming one's pubic hairs. There are women who completely shave their pubic hairs.

For Her

Should you shave your pubic area or just trim it? It's your decision. Some men find a cleanly shaven pubic area a real turn-on, but it can be uncomfortable for the woman. Whichever way you choose to go is okay. Do what you are comfortable with.

Some women have long, black wiry hairs growing around the areola of their nipples. This can be distasteful (sorry for the pun) for your husband. There is nothing wrong with regularly tweezing or trimming these hairs.

Do what you need to do to have the most enjoyable lovemaking experience possible!

Understanding Your Sexual Response Cycle

Dr. William H. Masters and Dr. Virginia E. Johnson, in their book *Human Sexual Response*, identified four stages in the sexual response cycle: the excitement phase, the plateau phase, the orgasmic phase, and the resolution phase.

Excitement

In the excitement phase your vagina begins to lubricate itself. There are many things that can begin this process. Sometimes a thought, a look from your husband, a smile, a touch, a word, or soothing music can cause you to automatically react with a pleasant feeling and the production of lubrication in the vagina.

Sometimes the vagina lubricates in reaction to external stimulation. Various foreplay activities can cause the vagina to lubricate. In younger women, lubrication often starts within 10–30 seconds after stimulation but in older women it can take 1–3 minutes.

Lubrication begins inside the vagina, high up inside. The natural moisture that the vagina produces has to work its way down through the vagina before it gets to the outer vaginal tissues. Knowing this, if a couple desires to speed up the movement of the lubricating fluid, the husband can reach up inside the vagina and help bring the lubricating fluid down to the outer tissues. When the outer tissues of the vagina are wet there is much more sexual pleasure for the wife. A wet vagina is a happy vagina! Other ways to wet the vagina's outer tissues are for the husband to lick his fingers and put his saliva on his wife's vaginal tissues, for the wife to do this for herself, or to use a sterile lubricant. These methods are especially helpful for the older woman.

One more way for the vaginal fluids to more easily make their way to the outer tissues is for the woman to change position. Gravity is a factor. Lying on her back there is no natural flow of these fluids toward the outside of the body. If a woman sits up or positions herself on top of her husband for a time, the lubricating fluids will flow naturally.

Low estrogen levels in women are responsible for vaginal dryness. This occurs during menopause and during breastfeeding. There are estrogen creams that can be rubbed into the vaginal tissues to increase hormonal levels. Talk with your doctor about any hormonal imbalances you may be concerned about. Make sure you tell him or her one of the reasons you're talking with him or her about this is because you're looking to maintain a great sex life!

Plateau

The plateau stage begins after lubrication and ends at orgasm. This stage can be long or short and can include waves of more and less intense sexual feelings. This can be the most pleasurable stage since it endures much longer than orgasm. This is where some of the greatest, most intense sexual experiences can occur for you. During the plateau stage, blood is trapped in the sexual organs and they have a heightened sensitivity to touch.

Sexual intensity and tension ebbs and flows until ultimately there is enough stimulation to produce orgasm.

Orgasm

At the orgasmic phase, the intense stimulation causes the clitoris, vulva, and vaginal tissues to begin the throbbing and pulsating contractions that are part of orgasm. Each contraction lasts about a second and the length of orgasm can vary from 6–15 throbs. Your heart beats faster, your breathing rate increases, and you might break into a serious sweat.

The feeling of orgasm begins in the clitoris or labia minora/vagina and can radiate throughout the whole body, even into the toes and the top of the head. This may not happen during every orgasm but it's possible.

 For Her

Want to have the most extraordinary sexual pleasure? Chart your menstrual cycle and plan your lovemaking time for about 13–17 days before your next anticipated menstruation. This is the time when you are ovulating and your body is just looking to get pregnant. So it is providing the best lubrication and sexual response possible to make that happen. BEWARE: This is also the time you're most likely to get pregnant so, if you don't want a baby in 9 months, use good protection!

Resolution

Women vary greatly from men in the resolution stage. For men, it may take hours after orgasm before the body is ready for another orgasm. This isn't true for women. For women, this period of time can be very short, even seconds or minutes. Women are capable of having multiple orgasms in a very short period of time.

 For Him

The time to really maximize your wife's sexual pleasure is during the plateau stage. This is where you have the potential to drive her crazy (so to speak). The longer this time is for her, the greater becomes her desire to spend lovemaking time with you.

Also, if she's tired she may not be able to reach orgasm but could still enjoy a lot of sexual pleasure in this stage and, when she's beat, it can be just as satisfying as orgasm.

Enjoying the Parts

Father God created us as sexual beings. We know that our sexual organs are not solely for procreation because of the fact that the woman's clitoris serves no other function than pleasure. It is not necessary for procreation. Father gave us our sexuality to enjoy. So how do we enjoy this gift?

Orgasm

Orgasm for you can be automatic but it is not necessarily so. For women there is a conscious and unconscious level by which orgasm may or may not happen. There are events in your life that may provide unconscious barriers to orgasm. When you are just plain exhausted you may not be able to get to orgasm no matter how hard you try.

Most women have no problem with their clitoris or labia minora/vagina responding sexually. When it's working right, the mere act of lovemaking can set it off and produce an orgasm. Some lovemaking positions vary in how effectively they stimulate the clitoris, so you may develop a preferred position for this reason. Experiences with orgasm vary from woman to woman. Women can get to orgasm in many different ways. Sometimes it's totally about the clitoris, sometimes it's totally about the vagina/labia minora and, believe it or not, I've known women who could reach orgasm through sensuous kissing with no genital touching whatsoever.

It's a wonderful thing when a husband and wife both orgasm together and it can and does happen, but it's actually not the norm. Some women report having orgasm with their husbands. Some women report that they can't orgasm with their husbands during intercourse. What this tells you is that between yourself and your husband, if you don't orgasm with him you have to orgasm before him or after him (or both). For women, it can vary from day to day.

Training the Clitoris

Some women need to actually "train" their clitoris because it doesn't seem to know what to do. This involves you touching yourself to discover what type of stimulation works for you to produce orgasm. Once you learn what works you can discuss it with your husband so that he can learn what you need. Most women can bring themselves to orgasm in less than 2 minutes. If you work to find out the kind of touch it takes to bring you to orgasm, you can train your husband to do it for you!

During lovemaking, as a woman's body goes through the different phases of sexual response, the clitoris changes in texture and size. It can become firm and erect, it can become soft, it can retreat further back into the body, and it can extend in length up to an inch.

Don't forget, there are two parts to the clitoris, the head and the glands. If the head becomes so sensitive to touch that the pleasure turns to pain, let your husband know that he can still tenderly touch the glands and you will get maximum pleasure.

 For Her

Get to know your body. Your body is a gift from God. It is beautiful no matter what it looks like because he made you. To be a woman is a wonderful and precious gift. God gave us our sexuality, anticipating that we would find what pleasures and joys it would bring to us in our covenanted relationship with our husbands. Don't rob yourself of the gift God gave you.

The Sleeping Orgasm

Men sometimes have wet dreams—sexual release as they sleep at night. What do women have? The sleeping orgasm. God made our bodies to need a physical connection with the opposite sex. It's this sex drive that brings us into marriage. When a couple makes love on a regular basis, neither husband nor wife will likely have a sleeping orgasm. However, there are times before marriage begins, after marriage ends, after death of a spouse, during times of sickness or times of marital stress where lovemaking is not possible. Our bodies are made for sexual intimacy and if sexual release doesn't come through lovemaking it will come through a sleeping orgasm.

Counseling a sexual abuse victim who had never had an orgasm with her husband revealed that she did have orgasms when she was asleep. This told her that her body was capable of having an orgasm. Also, from the sleeping orgasms, she came to know what an orgasm actually was (as she had no clue). Knowing that she could have an orgasm and what it was like, she was able to learn about her body and its functions and where and what it would take to get an orgasm while she was awake.

Women don't even need to be dreaming of anything sexual to have a sleeping orgasm. However, men most often have a sexually themed dream when they have a sleeping orgasm.

Dr. Truth

Remember, your clitoris serves no other purpose in your body than to bring you sexual pleasure!

Unconscious Barriers to Orgasm

Women need to have their minds engaged during lovemaking. For some women, they can't get to orgasm without very intense focus on the unity between themselves and their husband.

Because of negative, hurtful or abusive sexual contacts in the past, sometimes women unconsciously turn off their sexual responses. There are women who have never had an orgasm (before or without therapeutic intervention). If this is your situation, you probably need to engage a professional therapist to help you work through past hurts. Non-orgasmic women may need to literally train their bodies how to respond to sexual stimulation. It may not come naturally or spontaneously at all.

A woman hurt by sexual abuse may need to go through a year or two of therapy before she can begin to look at the sexual relationship with her husband. This type of book can feel very threatening to a victimized woman. When you have gone through a large part of your healing from abuse, you'll be able to pick this book up again and get much more out of it than you will now if you are unhealed.

 Word from the Wise

"Kiss me again and again, for your love is sweeter than wine. ... Take me with you. Come, let's run! Bring me into your bedroom ..." (Song of Songs 1:2,4)

Sexual love with your covenanted partner ought to be a wonderful, thrilling, fun, affirming, joy-filled adventure that starts with your vow and continues throughout married life. It is the sensuous pleasure you share with the one to whom your heart and soul are entwined as one.

How His Body Works

To look at them, you'd think men and women are really quite similar. And we are! Boys and girls have legs, arms, ankles, feet, hands, fingers, toes, ears, eyes, and assorted other body parts pretty much in equal portions. But there are some key differences.

It usually doesn't take a boy baby long to discover something really interesting between his legs, or a male toddler to realize he has something girls don't. Once this discovery is made, it almost seems as if all the other body parts disappear! We've already covered, or rather uncovered, the female parts. Now let's take a look, uh, talk about guy stuff.

The Parts and What They Do

Sometimes a cigar is just a cigar, but a penis is a lot more complex. The penis is composed primarily of spongy flesh: two areas called corpus cavernosa and one called corpus spongiosum. These areas are designed to fill with blood as the man becomes aroused; that's how an erection happens. Running down the middle of the penis is the urethra, a tube that channels both urine and semen from the body, though not at the same time.

Every penis looks a little different, including the angle it takes on when erect. This is determined by the ligament that is located at the base of the shaft of the penis where it is attached to the man's body. There's a good chance that when you got your first erection as a boy, your penis pointed slightly upward (when you were standing). Over the years, as the ligament sags a bit, the angle of erection may descend. Whatever the angle, it's all good and does not affect performance.

An exception to this rule is if the man is suffering from Peyronie's disease. If this is the case, the penis may be so curved (in any direction) when erect that it will not be comfortable or possible to engage in sex. Even before the penis shows signs of curving, erections are painful. If you believe you may have this problem, see a doctor, preferably a urologist. They can diagnose you and provide helpful treatment.

One young man who was about to get married was concerned because his penis was curved. He was worried that he wouldn't be able to have proper intercourse. He didn't have Peyronie's disease and was assured that even a curved penis could please one's wife. After the marriage, the young man confirmed that sex was not a problem. Just because his penis was curved didn't mean he had a medical problem.

The penis is topped by a cap called the glans. The opening at the tip of the glans is called the meatus while the edge of the cap is called the corona. The glans is very sensitive when the man is aroused as well as immediately after orgasm. When the penis is inserted in the vagina, by virtue of its shape it enhances the pleasure of the man and the woman. The glans is also appreciative of tender touching and kissing by the wife!

The glans will be covered by a foreskin when the penis is not erect if the man is uncircumcised. While myth says that sexual feeling is stronger in an uncircumcised penis since it is more protected when not in use, this is not true. What is true is that an uncircumcised male needs to spend a little more time on his hygiene.

Glands under the foreskin produce a discharge called smegma. If this discharge is not regularly cleaned away an infection or more serious problem can develop. When bathing or showering, you need to pull back your foreskin and thoroughly wash the head of your penis. Later, as you dry off, pull it back again and dry yourself gently. One young man, who had not practiced proper hygiene, awoke one morning with severe pain and a penis swollen more than twice its size—all because he had not taken proper care of his uncircumcised penis. Fortunately, a round of antibiotics got things right again.

Hanging below the base of the penis is the scrotum, which contains the testicles. When in the womb the testicles are inside the baby boy's body, and descend just prior to birth. Sometimes one or both testicles fail to make the descent. In these cases, at some point, medical intervention will be necessary.

Testicles produce testosterone as well as sperm. Sperm require a just-right temperature to survive, which is why the testicles hang outside the body. A testicle lodged in the body would be too warm to produce healthy sperm.

Word from the Wise

"After having sexual intercourse, both the man and the woman must bathe, and they will remain defiled until evening." (Leviticus 15:16-18)

God provided the children of Israel a detailed list of religious do's and don'ts, even related to sexual hygiene. Under the New Covenant, being ceremonially unclean is no longer an issue and we are not required to follow the old law. Sex, and the fluids it produces, do not defile us. Still, some of the ideas about hygiene are worthwhile.

Taking Care of the Parts

Like the young man mentioned above who woke up with an infected penis, too often men neglect to care for their bodies, including the parts they treasure most!

Good hygiene, whether you are circumcised or not, is an absolute requirement. Not only is hygiene healthy for you, but it is a courtesy toward your wife.

You may think that, since your penis is on the outside, it's naturally more clean and desirable when it comes to oral sex than your wife's vagina. Your wife might just have a different perspective.

Inside or outside is irrelevant. Since the most obvious use of a penis is to urinate, this can create a little discomfort for your wife. Also, guys, your crotch can get really sweaty and stinky. You need to keep yourself clean, whether you're circumcised or not.

In the shower, wash your penis, pubic hair, and anal area thoroughly with soap. Be sure to rinse completely, too. Out of the tub or shower, get yourself really dry.

For Him

Cleansing yourself before lovemaking honors your wife. You will be much more appealing if the sweat and dirt is washed off and your hair is clean. You also need to keep your fingernails and toenails trimmed. If you're touching her like you should be, long fingernails can hurt her, and toenails can gouge her. If you have long chest hairs, trim them, too. It will be much nicer for her to lay her head on your chest if hairs aren't poking up her nose! If you have a moustache, trim it also. It's a turn-off to be kissing your man and have his whiskers poking up your nose.

Other than cleanliness, you need to take care of your general health as well. Eating right, getting plenty of rest, and doing at least a little exercise (use the stairs instead of the elevator, taking the parking stall furthest from the door) will pay off in longer life and better sex.

Get regular physical check-ups. If something feels "off," go to the doctor. The old adage "better safe than sorry" is valid. We all know someone who looked the picture of health one day and only a few weeks or months later was dead from an otherwise non-fatal disease, the signs of which were ignored until it was too late. Keeping yourself healthy and visiting the doctor as needed will keep your wife happy. She'll feel more secure knowing you're in good health.

Understanding the Parts

Men know what a penis is for, but how all of their plumbing works remains a mystery until something starts going wrong. The penis is used to urinate, and, when erect and firm, for sexual intercourse. A man generally cannot urinate when fully aroused or ejaculate while urinating.

It's common for a man to wake up in the morning with an erection, when his testosterone levels are highest. Testosterone is produced in the testicles and is the male hormone responsible for sexual desire. It is testosterone that triggers voice and body changes in a boy at puberty, and puts hair on his face and other places.

He will also wake up needing to go to the bathroom, but he will need to wait until his penis softens before he can. However, if you begin feeling the need to urinate frequently, that could be sign of prostate problems. The prostate gland is located below the bladder and produces the fluid that makes semen look white. It wraps around the urethra and is about the size of a walnut. In most men, as you age your prostate enlarges, squeezing the urethra. You will feel the need to urinate more frequently and maybe more urgently. There is no cause for alarm unless you experience other symptoms such as burning while urinating, painful ejaculation, difficulty starting and stopping urination, and excessive (disruptive to your sleep) night time urination.

Prostatitis is an infection of the prostate that yields fever, painful urination, pain in the area of your scrotum, and lower back pain. These symptoms mean you need to see the doctor. An occasional twinge of pain in the testicles that fades after several seconds is not unusual and is nothing to be alarmed about.

The testicles are composed of a complex maze of seminiferous tubules that are organized in more than two hundred compartments. Sperm are manufactured in the tubules, which are connected to epididymis, which is connected to the vas deferens, which empties into the urethra. A vasectomy involves severing and tying off the cut ends of the vas deferens.

Two problems can be centered in a man's testicles. If you and your wife are experiencing difficulty getting pregnant, your sperm count may be low. The causes for this could be many and you need to see a doctor for diagnosis. Another issue is connected to aging. Testosterone levels often fall as a man ages. Usually this does not create a problem. However, if you are feeling more than reasonably tired all the time and your libido (sexual desire) slips, you may need hormone replacement treatments. Again, consult your doctor for a proper diagnosis and treatment plan.

 For Her

Generally, men hate to hear of problems that result from aging and illness. Partly this stems from their sense of machismo. And partly it's due to fear. A man's mantra could be "What you don't know can't hurt you." Gently but persistently encourage your husband to see the doctor regularly for check-ups and anytime something isn't working right. Let him know that his health is something you have a right to know about since you want to keep him around for a long time.

Understanding Your Sexual Response Cycle

Dr. William H. Masters and Dr. Virginia E. Johnson, in their book *Human Sexual Response* identified four stages in the sexual response cycle: the excitement phase, the plateau phase, the orgasmic phase, and the resolution phase.

Excitement

In the excitement phase a man's penis becomes erect. There are many things that can begin this process. Sometimes a thought, a look from his wife, a smile, a touch, a word, or soothing music can cause the man to automatically react with a sexual response and the development of an erection. Therefore physical or emotional excitement can begin this phase. The penis becomes engorged with blood, and then erect. The penis can remain erect for extended periods of time as long as there is ongoing and varied stimulation and ejaculation doesn't occur.

An erection can be lost before ejaculation but can often be brought back. Anxiety can cause a man to lose his erection. Nonsexual events can occur to cause the loss of your erection (phone rings, child knocks on door, wife says something during sex that makes you mad). Men can also get nipple erections at this phase. As well, the testicles will swell a little, the scrotum tightens and thickens and lubricating fluid may appear.

Plateau

During the plateau stage, blood is trapped in the penis, the heart rate continues to go up, respiration continues to increase, blood pressure increases, and your skin begins to flush. Your testicles will withdraw up into your scrotum. A small amount of pre-ejaculatory fluid may be secreted. You might experience muscle spasms in your hands, feet, and face. Muscle tension increases. The size of the testicles is noticeably increased and seminal fluid begins collecting around the prostate gland.

The plateau stage can be rather short or rather long. This depends on the emotional intensity and desire experienced by each person. Pleasure and tension increase throughout the plateau stage until orgasm is reached.

Orgasm

At the orgasmic phase, sufficient intense stimulation causes pulsating muscular contractions. Each contraction lasts about a second and the length of orgasm can be 5—6 throbbing contractions (the second and third ones are the most intense). It is these rhythmic contractions that cause the ejaculate to be released. Your sphincter muscles tighten and prohibit any urine from being released while at the same time stopping any ejaculate from draining backwards into the bladder. A man generally knows when he reaches the point of no return and ejaculation is inevitable. You can't do anything to stop it at this point. The younger you are, the more forceful the ejaculation. With age, the forcefulness decreases.

Your heart beats faster, your breathing rate increases, and breaking into a serious sweat is common. At ejaculation your face will grimace, your feet will spasm, every muscle is engaged for a forceful release of sexual tension. Engorged blood is released, the man ejaculates.

Did you remember that sex begins in the brain? Yes, that initial stimulation (physical or mental) causes the brain to send chemical messages to the penis that cause blood to start flowing into the penis bringing on an erection. Well, for the man it ends in the brain too. All that sexual stimulation causes chemical messages to go to the brain which then sends messages back to the penis giving it the signal to ejaculate.

Some men experience post-ejaculation pain in the glans (head of the penis). If this is true for you, let your wife know so that she doesn't irritate your penis unknowingly.

Resolution

During resolution the body returns to its normal state. This happens very quickly for men. The penis becomes flaccid again, the scrotum thins and drops, the testes drop down and return to normal size, the skin perspires, the muscles relax, engorgement is relieved. After resolution there must be a rest period before arousal begins again. This is called the refractory period.

For young men, the refractory period (period of time before orgasm is possible again) may be only a few minutes or a few hours. But, it isn't long before the "few minutes" in refractory time is gone forever and then the waiting time will at least be a few hours. The older you get, the greater the time period grows between orgasmic possibilities. Refractory time varies among men.

After orgasm you may feel fatigue along with a sense of contentment and well-being. This is a time for "afterglow" with your wife.

Dr. Truth

Once and for all, size does not matter! If you've got about two inches of erect penis, that's all your wife needs for her pleasure. The outer section of her vagina is about an inch and a half deep. These are the muscles that contract during orgasm. When her muscles contract they grab hold of your penis. The only part she'll feel of your penis is the first inch and a half! That's it. The rest of her vagina has virtually no feeling, so it doesn't matter how deep penetration is. So, with a couple of erect inches, both you and your wife will be able to experience a thoroughly satisfying sex life. Bigger is just different and not necessarily better.

Enjoying the Parts

It usually doesn't take a baby boy long to discover his penis and make the connection that touching it feels good. Such self-touching is normal. Even occasional masturbation as the boy grows up is to be expected and should be tolerated.

When is masturbation a bad thing? For some Christians, all masturbation is bad. Period. Yet there is nothing in the Bible to support this view. What is in the Bible are guidelines for proper sexual behavior and thought. Masturbation becomes a problem when it is obsessive and addictive, and when what you think about or look at while doing it is sinful. Lusting after women (other than your wife if you are married), becoming aroused while thinking of being sexual with them, and looking at pornography, puts you in the danger zone of sin. This is not appropriate behavior or thinking for a Christian man of any age.

It isn't uncommon at all. But it is wrong. If this is a problem area for you, talk to your pastor or a male counselor. Deal with the issue quickly before it becomes a lifelong and destructive obsession.

If masturbation is infrequent and you don't look at pornography or fantasize about sex, you're probably okay. Keep in mind, your body will naturally get its own sexual release as often as it needs it whether you are married or not. Nocturnal emissions occur when the body needs a release. Men most often are dreaming about sexual things when they have sleeping orgasms (women can be dreaming about anything). See Chapter 9 for more information about masturbation. Feel free to talk with your pastor or a friend of the same sex if you're feeling uncertain about the appropriateness of what you're doing.

What about mutual masturbation while dating? For teens, it is hands off the genital regions at all times! No sexual touching should occur, not even of the breasts or through clothing. Hold hands, kiss, and put your arms around each other's waist. Beyond that, draw the line and protect your purity. In fact, this is the right policy for every dating situation regardless of age.

For Her

A man's penis generally needs a good deal more vigorous stimulation than does your clitoris, but that doesn't mean the penis isn't sensitive. The glans and the underside of the penis just below the glans are very sensitive areas where you will want to touch a bit more gently. But feel free to wrap your hand firmly around the shaft of the erect penis and pump up the volume! Use steady rhythmic strokes and allow your husband to cue you as to speed. The older your husband gets, the more direct stimulation of the penis he will need and desire.

Sex is a potent force. Once the desires are stirred and the passion is at full steam, the urge for sexual release becomes nearly overwhelming. The most holy, pure, well intentioned "goody-goody" people have been brought down by playing around with sex.

If you stoke the fire you will get burned. For Christians, purity is a requirement, not an option. Sex (oral, vaginal, anal, manual) is wrong outside of marriage.

The point of sexual touching (foreplay) is preparation for intercourse. Intercourse is a special relationship reserved exclusively for people married to each other.

Some engaged couples tell themselves that they will be getting married and have already made that commitment to each other, so why can't they start sexual intercourse now? Let's make this perfectly clear—there is no such thing as a private marriage. Marriage is a public, legal event done before witnesses (this is true for every culture in the world!). No culture on earth purports legitimacy of "secret marriage." You aren't married until you're married. Period! As a wise man once said, "Just because they're engaged, doesn't mean they'll get married."

Sex outside of marriage is sin no matter how you try to dress it up. And many things can happen in life—you might not actually marry the person you're engaged to. Lots of people are engaged a number of times before they get married. Keep yourselves pure. Don't be deceived by the evil one.

As a mature, Christian adult, it's your decision how to behave with your beloved. Whatever you do, don't do it without a careful reading of your Bible and a lot of prayer. Keeping your spiritual life strong and healthy is the best way to keep your sexual life strong and healthy, before and after marriage!

Word from the Wise

"Do not let sin control the way you live; do not give in to its lustful desires. Do not let any part of your body become a tool of wickedness, to be used for sinning. Instead, give yourselves completely to God since you have been given new life." (Romans 6:12,13)

The words "any part of your body" don't refer just to your sex organs. As a Christian you are called to use every part of your body (your whole being) in God's service. You avoid lying with your lips, hurting with your hands, lusting with your mind, and deceiving with your actions. Focus your thoughts on holiness and show tenderness to your spouse as evidence of God's grace.

Chapter

8

Preparation: Mind, Body, Heart, and Soul

Sexual intercourse doesn't just happen. Great sex in marriage occurs when the beforeplay is ongoing!

What's beforeplay? That's what goes on between a man and a woman before they engage in foreplay. It involves the quality of regular daily interactions, including personal hygiene, courtesy, compliments, loving behavior, and on and on. Every time you are nice to your spouse, you are engaging in beforeplay.

Men are turned on more by visual stimulation and women by touch and words. A wife who cares for herself and her body is attractive and inviting to her husband. A husband who speaks gently and lovingly to his wife, caressing her arm, touching her hand, will draw his wife's interest.

There are sights, sounds, and smells involved in the mating dance which are part and parcel of the entire sexual experience. Being aware of these turn-ons can enhance any couple's sex life.

Getting Ready for Intimacy

WebMD Medical News reported in February 2002 that a survey of 1,500 men reported that it takes men about an hour from the time they first think of sex to when they are actually engaging in intercourse, and that sex for men may not be as spontaneous as people have thought.

> "Men typically ponder the idea of having sex for about 28 minutes before they make the decision to go for it. Once they've decided it seems like the thing to do, it takes them another 14 minutes to actually start foreplay. Foreplay lasts about 12-14 minutes before taking it to the next level."

One wonders if they had done this study with women what the findings would have been. Let's say they would have been similar. If there are 28 minutes from the time a person first thinks about sex to the point they make a decision that they want to try to pursue sex with their spouse, and another 14 minutes between that moment and the start of foreplay, we have a lot of time to work with!

Most people don't have hours and hours of time for sex unless they are on their honeymoon, on vacation (without kids), or the kids have finally left home to live on their own. An hour for sex for people who are working, have kids, and other things to do seems fairly reasonable and typical.

Unlike animals that mate merely from instinct, we can decide to make love just because we want to. We can decide to make love any time we want to, which is not dependant on any season or optimum conception period. (The panda bear is only fertile two or three days per year. Since they have sex only by instinct to reproduce, they have sex only once a year, if a male is available in the vicinity at the optimal time.)

How do we get ready for intimacy? In our mind, body, heart, and soul.

Mind

We feel the orgasm in our physical bodies but the road to intimacy starts long before. It starts in our minds.

Every sex therapist will tell you that sex is all about the mind. The largest sex organ is the brain. Aside from the fact that all hormones related to our sexual functioning reside in the brain or are controlled by the brain, it's more than hormones. Sex has a distinct mental element.

We already learned that a man spends around 28 minutes thinking about lovemaking before he makes his first move. The mind is the first thing to be engaged before lovemaking. We get ready for intimacy by first turning our minds toward intimacy and thinking about it.

Our bodies are not just acting on instinct. Most of the sex we will have with our spouses won't be to try to produce children. Rather, it will be because we desire to share ourselves intimately with each other. Sex will start in our minds, with a decision.

Whether or not we proceed into intimacy is all about the decisions we make in our minds. This is where previous or current fights or arguments can interfere with intimacy. This is where bringing up issues about the kids can interfere with intimacy. This is where unhealed emotional scars from abuse can interfere with intimacy. This is where we decide if we have felt loved and are cared about enough to want to share ourselves with our spouses.

This thinking prepares our bodies for intimacy. As we think about lovemaking with our spouse, our body begins to respond.

If our minds are not engaged fully in intimacy with our spouses, our spouse will feel it. It will feel to your spouse as if they are making love to a mannequin. But this is not making love—this is a marriage that needs special help from a qualified mental health therapist.

Body

Only after our minds are engaged in thinking about intimacy does our body begin to respond and desire intimacy. For men, thinking about intimacy usually causes the penis to become erect. For women, thinking about intimacy will start the vagina lubricating.

Greasy hair, stinky breath, and serious body odor are real turn-offs. Out of respect for each other we owe it to our spouse to keep our body clean. If we keep them clean regularly we will be hygienically desirable to our spouse should we become intimate.

Refer to Chapters 6 and 7 for specific things men and women should do to keep their bodies ready for intimacy (you know, like trimming toenails!).

Heart

Our heart is where we experience our feelings, our emotions, and our desires. After we are thinking about intimacy and we have our body prepared for intimacy, we prepare our heart by thinking specifically about our spouse and the love we share together as a couple. When we think of special things we have done together, special things our spouse has done for us, some of the good times we've had, we are preparing our heart to welcome our spouse in intimacy.

It is important for a couple to create good memories for this reason. The other reason is that when you're fighting and feel like ditching your spouse, having the good things to recall may play a huge role in helping you to see that the fight is temporary and that there is more to your marriage than this fight, which will pass!

Our heart is engaged when we think about the past, the present, and the future that we have with the one we love, the one we've committed our lives to, the one we will grow old with, our partner, our companion, our confident.

One woman had trouble with sexual stimulation and orgasm. She discovered that, during sex, if she really focused her thoughts on how much she loved her husband and the unity they had together, she could come to orgasm. For her, it took an intentionally focused mind to get to orgasm.

Sometimes just thinking of the intimacy that is about to happen helps us to feel a heart link to our lover, our spouse.

Soul

Preparing the soul for intimacy involves our spiritual lives, of course. How do we prepare our soul?

As Christians it is the steady pursuit throughout our lives to walk a life of sanctification. We are continually working to grow the fruit of the spirit in our lives. Personally we need to be keeping short accounts with the Lord and we need to be seeking intimacy with God. With the Lord's grace and mercy, it is our obligation to seek healing for the brokenness in our lives. As we heal, our souls gain peace.

For Him

As the spiritual head of your home, take the initiative to pray with your wife daily. This does not have to take a lot of time. It can be as simple as each saying a couple of sentences in prayer for one another. Here's a simple formula:

Express thanks for one good quality your wife possesses or a specific act that she has done (like cooking a great meal the night before).

Pray God's blessing, protection, and enablement on your wife as a covering for her day.

Next, it's your wife's turn to pray for you.

Married Christian couples must pray for each other daily! It can be short and sweet but it must be a priority.

Marriages are under attack every day from the kingdom of darkness. The enemy loves nothing better than to destroy Christian marriages. Covens of witches are known to specifically take time to curse Christian marriages. We need to pray for our marriages, daily and together. The enemy wins when he can divide and conquer. Don't let this happen to your marriage.

A great way to start your day is lying in bed cuddled up together. Have your morning coffee together in bed, and then pray for each other before heading out to your day. The husband can pray for the wife, and the wife for the husband. The husband can then pray a covering prayer over the family, home, and marriage as the wife agrees.

At day's end, cuddle up again! Sit in bed or together on your couch and cuddle. Chat a bit about your day while enjoying a little snack. No matter what kind of a day you've had, whether there has been conflict or not, bring your marriage into a state of peace before you go to sleep, whether you have sex that night or not.

Word from the Wise

"And 'don't sin by letting anger gain control over you.' Don't let the sun go down while you are still angry, for anger gives a mighty foothold to the Devil." (Ephesians 4:26-27)

Don't allow anger to tear your marriage apart, not even for a day. Strive to make things right with each other as the day draws to an end. Come together and begin to pray and give thanks to God for everything you have and ask for his grace and his forgiveness to come to you both and soften your hearts.

When our souls are cluttered, distressed, in pain, or oppressed, our experience of intimacy is not all that it can be. Sometimes, sex is just sex in these circumstances.

Our souls need to be cared for every day. When our souls are at peace sex takes on a whole other dimension. After our minds are engaged and our bodies are ready and our hearts are joined, what makes our lovemaking experience all that it can be is the connection of our souls, one to another.

In Genesis 2:24 we read "and the two are united into one." At the height of our intimate sexual experience and directly thereafter, it is our souls that meld together and connect with each other.

Making Time for Intimacy

Making time for intimacy may seem silly to newlyweds, but those who have been married for a while know the value of making time for your intimate life. When we make time for intimacy we develop the marriage and continue to take it to deeper levels.

One of the biggest issues for couples is that they are doing too much all the time and are too exhausted when together. Making time for intimacy isn't just about finding a time to have sex—it's about taking care of your energy level and your health on a daily or weekly basis so that you can have sex when you find the time. It's pitiful when you have the time booked and arrangements for kids made and then you're both so exhausted you just want to go to sleep.

It is disheartening to see programs on TV about couples trying to get pregnant and failing because they are dual career couples and their biggest problem is that they never have time to be together (sometimes they are only at home together a few days per month). They have to try to make specific appointments together during her most fertile days and then try to have sex on those days. When they get together they are so exhausted that sex isn't even fun, it's a chore.

Dr. Truth

In the Old Testament, men and women were forbidden to engage in sex during a woman's period. That is part of the law that has passed away. Today it is entirely a matter of personal preference. Sex during menstruation may be a tad messier but can still be just as rewarding as at any other time. You may want to place a towel under the woman to prevent any staining. Otherwise, there is no medical or moral reason to not have sex during a woman's periods.

Since sexual intimacy is something that needs to be developed and nurtured in your marriage, you need to see it as something that requires the investment of your time and energy. We plan for a lot of things in life, vacations, medical appointments, kids' programs at school, socializing with friends, going to church, or meeting a friend for lunch. Why would we think that allotting time for sexual intimacy with our spouses wouldn't be as important as any of these?

There will always be moments when we're just together in bed with our spouse and we'll just warm up to each other and make love. Sweet! Then there will be times when we take care of some of our spouse's chores, when we take them away from the grind, when we let them know that we want to make them the focus of our evening. We might unplug the phone, turn off the TV, turn on the music, light the fireplace, and fix some snacks and nice drinks and focus on each other for the evening and begin the lovemaking long before we get to bed. Sweeter!

Those who have small children have a special challenge. Being able to be alone in your bedroom and have energy is nothing but a small miracle. Couples who have the least amount of sex and the least amount of marital satisfaction are those with preschool children. Couples with small children have to do more to keep their marriage alive. Use every resource you have to provide you with sleeping time and alone time. Mothers who are at home with preschool children need sleep first, sex second. If you value sex with your wife you'll take over the kids often enough that you let her get her rest!

Conversely, couples reporting the greatest marital satisfaction are those who have not had kids yet and those who never had kids. As kids get older and start leaving home, married couples' level of reported marital satisfaction slowly increases but never reaches the level of satisfaction that the childless couples have. This makes a lot of sense. It has to do with the time and energy available for the marriage (intimacy included).

Make time for your intimate life. You will reap the rewards, even if there are kids around. It's never too late to buck the statistics, either!

Getting Psyched for Intimacy

In Philippians 4:8-9, Paul writes, "Fix your thoughts on what is true and honorable and right. Think about things that are pure and lovely and admirable. " And in Romans 8:6, he writes, "If your sinful nature controls your mind, there is death. But if the Holy Spirit controls your mind, there is life and peace."

So what does all of this thinking have to do with sex? How you think about sex with your spouse, and how you think about your spouse will affect the quality of your sex life with him or her.

If you harbor anger toward your spouse on a continual basis, over time you will desire having sex with them less and less. This is something that needs to be forgiven and released. Talk to your spouse.

If you are always fantasizing about a relationship with someone else, over time sex with your spouse will become less satisfying. Longing sexually or romantically for any man or woman who is not your spouse is a sin. Put up your guard. Pray for strength and a pure heart. Refocus your heart on your spouse and only your spouse.

If there is something that bothers you that your spouse does when you make love and you fail to discuss it, it will plague your mind and make sex less desirable. Talk to your spouse about the issue.

If you have any negative issues with sex or your sexuality, these will weigh on your mind and bog down your sexual relationship with your spouse. These need to be addressed with a therapist so that your mind can instead focus on the positive aspects of sex.

Most of us have probably heard that an act of sin starts in the mind. What we sometimes fail to recognize is that positive actions also start in the mind.

If you want to have great sex with your husband or wife, start thinking about having great sex with them! Yearn for him or her deeply. Song of Songs 3:1 says, "One night as I lay in bed, I yearned deeply for my lover …." Think about all the possible places and ways you two could enjoy making love. Plan a spousal seduction in your mind. Enjoy playing with the thoughts of kissing, touching, disrobing, fondling, and making love with your spouse. Let these kinds of thoughts about your spouse run rampant in your mind—and then do it! Make your imaginings come true when you're together.

Thinking sexy thoughts about your really hot husband or wife is a crucial part of beforeplay. Indulge yourself and then indulge them.

Word from the Wise

"Come quickly, my love! Move like a swift gazelle or a young deer on the mountains of spices." (Song of Songs 8:14)

A husband and wife making love is a blessed and biblical act. It is holy and profound. And nowhere in the Bible are there any restrictions on positions in passion. Be a gazelle or be a deer, but enjoy those mountains of spice.

Getting Thrilled with Intimacy

You've gotten ready. You've made time. You've been thinking hot thoughts about your spouse all day. Now the time has come for you to come! Well, almost.

Don't rush it or force it. Relish every aspect of your sexual encounter with your spouse. After beforeplay comes foreplay! This is where the thoughts turn to touching, stroking, kissing, sucking, licking, teasing, rubbing … you get the picture.

For Her

Find out what turns your man on and provide it! You may prefer silk nighties while he finds flannel PJ's really sexy. You may hate flannel, but wearing it once in awhile, especially on a cold winter night, won't kill you. If that's his turn-on, you won't be wearing it long anyway!

The same is true for positions. Try what he would like to try, as long as it does not make you feel totally uncomfortable. If you're merely feeling a little reluctant, let go and give it a shot. You may find you really like the suggestion, or he may discover it wasn't as good as he thought it would be. You'll never know until you try.

Take your time. Men, linger over your wife's body. Gently run your fingers along her back, hips, legs, thighs, and arms. Kiss her all over. Feel her skin against your skin. Don't rush to fondle her clitoris. Spend some time with her nipples and the rest of her body first.

Women, take hold of your man's penis. He's ready for your touch right away, even if it's just holding his penis gently in your hand before you begin to stroke him. Nuzzle his neck and stroke his chest. Wrap your arms around him and massage his lower back a little. When you're ready, take his hand and place it on your vagina and press his fingers. Let him know now is the time to take the foreplay to the next level. Later, again when you're ready, open your legs and pull him toward you.

Enjoy together every sweet aspect of the blessing and holy communion of marital sex.

Chapter 9

Doing It: Part 1

Finally, we're getting to the "good" part of sex, actually doing it!
Are you ready? If not, read on and you will be!

Romancing

Ah, romancing. Remember the four stages in the sexual response
cycle: the excitement phase, the plateau phase, the orgasmic phase,
the resolution phase? Romancing comes right at the beginning. It is
romancing that causes our bodies to begin to respond sexually and
the excitement phase begins. Remember how sex begins in the
mind? Remember how it's been found that most men (and probably women) spend 28 minutes thinking about sex before making
their first move and then 14 minutes before foreplay starts? This is
where the romancing comes in.

Romancing starts in the mind of either you or your spouse. It
will stay there unless you do something, right? Right! If you start
thinking about sex you then need to decide if you want to try to
"get lucky" with your spouse and have a time of intimacy together.
Now, just because you're interested, you're not sure if they are!
Here comes the fine art and finesse of determining whether or not
your spouse is interested, in the mood, has energy, might want to
get interested, or just wants to be left alone. This is when the fear
of rejection or history of rejection might come in to play and where
ongoing communication with your spouse is critical. Sometimes

there is no way at all to guess whether your husband or wife might like some physical intimacy. You're going to have to either start talking or start romancing.

It will be easier for him or her to get in the mood if he or she doesn't have chores and duties to take care of. What can you help with? Is he or she stressed? What helps him or her unwind? What can you do for him or her?

For some women, romancing is really important, for others, it doesn't matter a hill of beans. There are lots of women who have such a positive attitude about sex and so little negative sexual baggage that if you're interested, they're happy to know it and happy to do it right here, right now!

If your wife's sexual history includes abuse or some other type of wounding, you may have to do much more work to get to intimacy. Wounded women may need to know exactly what you want, how you want to do it, when you want it, and where you want it. Wounded women can't easily handle spontaneous sexual advances even from their loving husbands because it feels much too out of control for them. The only relaxed sex they can have is when they know all the parameters of the sexual activity before it happens. The unexpected for them adds to their pain and fear.

Sometimes we might be interested in intimacy but it's just not a good time. We can see that our spouse is tired, sick, totally engaged in his or her favorite TV show, cooking dinner, or maybe they aren't even home at the time. However, we can't presume that just because our spouse is engaged in something that they wouldn't like to hear that we are interested to share some intimacy a little later on. Remember, get them thinking about it in advance.

What does romancing "look" like? Nearly anything. Romancing is when you make your overtures to your spouse to let them know you're interested in lovemaking. It may come in a glance, a squeeze, a sensuous kiss, lighting of candles in the bedroom, little suggestions or statements of interest, or little questions of your spouse to see if they might like to fool around.

Keep in mind, these little things might not mean anything other than your spouse is doing something nice for you. There may be no sexual innuendo intended at all. This is where we need to "talk" with each other. Make your interests known verbally. People can get really good at reading each other's signals but sometimes the signals get crossed and sometimes we're just plain wrong in our interpretations of what we think the other person is trying to tell us. Remove all doubt and "talk."

Word from the Wise

"Young Woman: 'The king is lying on his couch, enchanted by the fragrance of my perfume. My lover is like a sachet of myrrh lying between my breasts. He is like a bouquet of flowers in the gardens of En-gedi.'

Young Man: 'How beautiful you are, my beloved, how beautiful! Your eyes are soft like doves.'

Young Woman: 'What a lovely, pleasant sight you are, my love, as we lie here on the grass, shaded by cedar trees and spreading firs.'" (Song of Songs 1:12-16)

Mmm, sweet romance. Don't let the romance fade out of your marriage. Don't let intimacy become totally predictable. Be creative. You will never be too old to sit under the shade of a tree and tell your spouse what a pleasant sight they are to you!

A little teasing, a little squeezing, a little nuzzling, or a little smile can be very simple.

Of course, there is also elaborate romancing. Taking your spouse out for dinner, theatre, a carriage ride, or a movie might be part of the romancing. Just don't forget, the older you get, the more tired you get and by the time you get home you may be too pooped for passion in the bedroom. Sometimes even when you're younger a late night can do you in physically.

Romancing involves setting the ambience and tone for your intimacy. Bright lights might be great for exploring outside but can be intimidating and uncomfortable in the bedroom. Soft and subdued lighting is romantic. Candles can provide soft lighting. Put 25- or 50-watt bulbs in a lamp or two. A fireplace can provide enough light on its own.

Aromatherapy has its benefits. The smell of vanilla is said to be very relaxing and tranquil. Feeding each other blueberries or strawberries can be a sensual activity.

Fresh clean sheets are always nice to be in, but when you're really hot to trot it doesn't matter what kind of condition the sheets are in!

Foreplay

Remember the plateau stage of the sexual response cycle? This is the stage where sexual tension and stimulation increases steadily until orgasm is on the immediate horizon. Everything you do to touch each other after mutual interest has been ascertained is foreplay. "Fore" is that which comes before, "play" is play. Play before orgasm, get it? Also, we need to play to get to orgasm!

How do we play? Not all play is equally arousing. In fact, some can be downright painful or can do us some damage. We're talking about loving and focused touching, kissing, caressing, stimulating, sucking, pumping, and rubbing.

Foreplay has also been referred to as petting or necking. While foreplay can begin with nonsexual touching it always builds to include direct touching of each other's sexual organs. The point of foreplay is to stimulate the sexual response in each other's body in preparation for sexual intercourse. This is another reason why engaging in petting or necking or any other foreplay-like activity outside of marriage is wrong. Once the body's sexual triggers have been pulled, so to speak, the need to "get off" can temporarily block out the moral sensibilities, especially in males, and insist on release.

Inside of marriage, foreplay can be a lot of fun. Every couple will develop their own foreplay game plans that best fit their personalities. Everyone is different. There is no absolute right or wrong way to go about foreplay. As newlyweds, you'll experiment with different touches, timings, and so on until you find those actions that you are both comfortable with and that are stimulating for you.

A typical foreplay scenario could go like this: You and your spouse are in the living room cuddling. You kiss a bit and decide to make love. You go into your bedroom (especially if there are kids around), get undressed (or undress each other), and get under the covers (or not). You hold each other, enjoying the feel of skin on skin, and kiss and stroke each other's body.

All the senses are engaged. As you each become aroused, the woman takes the man's penis in her hand and gently strokes it. He leans down and kisses her breasts, sucking gently on her nipples, while his hand moves to her pelvis area. Very gently his fingers find her clitoris and very gently begins massaging.

From here, there are any number of actions available to you. Here are just a few examples. Feel free to explore, experiment, and add to the list!

Oral Sex

There is nothing inherently sinful in oral sex. It can be fun and even an alternative to intercourse. The key is to be comfortable with it. Neither partner should ever coerce the other into engaging in any activity they are not comfortable with. If engaging in oral sex, it's a good idea to wash your genital area quickly before getting into bed. Simply wiping your penis or vagina with a warm washcloth can be adequate.

Giving Your Wife Oral Sex

A husband performing oral sex on his wife needs to be gentle and go slowly. Part the vaginal lips with your fingers and lubricate her. Run your tongue up and down inside her vulva. Excite the clitoris with circular tongue motions, and even gently suck on the clitoris and hold it between your lips (but no biting or nibbling!). It can be very erotic for your wife to even put your whole face in her vulva. A pointy tongue may be irritating to her. A fully wide, soft tongue may drive her wild with excitement. Your nose can even stimulate her clitoris while your mouth is fully licking and stimulating her vulva. Long slow licks with the tongue provide maximum contact, producing the most pleasure for your wife. Let your lips fully engage her soft tissues. Stimulating the clitoris while making full contact with the labia minora is incredibly pleasurable for your wife.

To add to her titillation, reach up to her breasts with both hands, hold firmly with a wide open hand and massage firmly. She might enjoy you gently squeezing her nipples. Her nipples could be too sensitive for that and could produce pain. She should tell you if it hurts and redirect you to what would feel better for her. If you can touch both her nipples with one hand and place the other hand just above her pubic bone and apply a little pressure, she'll be in complete ecstasy.

If you're going to give her oral sex, take her all the way to orgasm with it. She'll be smiling in her sleep all night! Since women can have multiple orgasms easily in one lovemaking adventure, giving her an orgasm orally won't detract from vaginal intercourse for her or you. Of course, even if you give her a little oral sex to help her get moistened, she'll enjoy every bit of it.

Blowing on your wife's vaginal area while she is wet and moist adds pleasure for her. If you are manually stimulating her, add some lubricant and turn on the ceiling fan while you masturbate her. She'll love it!

You can purchase flavored lubricants that will get warm or hot when breathed on or rubbed. Some women will easily get yeast infections from these lubricants because they upset a woman's pH balance in the vagina. However, if these lubricants don't bother your wife and give her more pleasure and you like the taste, use them. You will find, though, that your wife has a nice flavor on her own without additives.

Giving Your Husband Oral Sex

A woman performing oral sex on a man needs to be aware of where her teeth are! Generally, you want to keep your teeth away from the penis, especially the head (glans), which is very sensitive. As you take the penis into your mouth, moisten it with ample saliva or water based lubricant. (You can run out of saliva.) Run your tongue over the head and up and down the underside of the shaft. Take as much of the penis into your mouth as you are comfortable with and suck gently. Think of sucking and licking a popsicle (but no biting!)—the same kind of attention to your husband's penis will drive him wild. You may also want to stroke the base of the shaft as you hold the top of the penis in your mouth.

It's a bit of an experiment for a woman to find out how much of her husband's penis she can handle having in her mouth. We all have a natural gag reflex that will kick in when your throat is trying to protect itself. It is a learned skill for women to receive a full penis in their mouths. Most erect penises are in the 5 to 6 inch range; of course, your mouth is only 2 to 3 inches deep. It's possible to allow your husband's penis to slip part way into your throat if you are able to control your gag reflex. Some women just can't do this but those who can do it say it is very much a learned skill, a mind over matter thing. Your husband won't get any additional pleasure from this. It's pornography that has told men that this is what they want or should try to get. It's not necessary and this is a deception.

A man with a full erection of 3 to 4 inches will have the most satisfying oral sex because his wife will likely be able to receive his full penis in her mouth.

While you have as much of the end of his penis in your mouth as you are comfortable with, firmly grasp the lower part of his penis with your hand and provide a pumping motion. Your hand should touch your lips so that his complete penis is being touched. Synchronize your hand and mouth so that when your hand goes down you are sucking his penis into your mouth and when your hand travels up the shaft of his penis, you are releasing the glans to slide downward out of your mouth. Short sucking actions are better than a long vacuum cleaner method. However, don't let the glans leave your mouth, they are traveling solely within your closed mouth. Don't forget that you'll give him extra pleasure if you twist your hand one way going down and the other way going up. For a little variety now and then, warm your mouth with hot tea, cool it with ice chips, hum while you suck, or prep your mouth with cool mints before your receive the glans of his penis.

With your free hand he will probably enjoy you playing with his testicles or gently scratching them. Remember, be gentle with the testicles! Another area to stimulate is his perineum. This is the muscle between his anus and his testicles. If you apply a little pressure on that spot during oral sex (or other manual stimulation) he will be in the height of ecstasy! If you aren't playing with his balls, play with his pubic hair with the other hand. Let him feel as much bodily sensation as possible all at the same time.

It's not necessary for a wife to swallow the ejaculate. That's all about personal preference. Men ought not to expect it or think this is the way it's done. If your wife is giving you oral sex of her own volition, she needs to make this decision herself. You will be able to detect how close he is to ejaculation because you'll see his reactions to you. If you sense he is very close, you can switch to masturbating him with your hands or slide his penis into your vagina for him to finish. You can also let him come into your hands. Some women will let their husbands come in their mouths but not swallow. You will know that the first contraction is happening if your thumbs are at the base of his penis because you can feel the contractions of orgasm beginning.

You can gently lift up his testicles, gently encourage him to lift up his knees, then lick his perineum. See how he likes that! He may also enjoy you tickling him with your tongue just under the frenulum (the V-shaped section of the glans just under the urethral opening). Licking the underside of his penis in up and down strokes with your tongue will also bring him pleasure. Allowing one of his testicles at a time slip into your mouth will probably be appreciated—but gentle down there!

You can start oral sex with your husband while he is still soft or wait until he is erect. He'll enjoy it either way.

For both sexes, be aware that as arousal increases so does sensitivity to touch in the nipples, penis, and clitoris. Be aware and be gentle. If something is uncomfortable, gently let your spouse know so they can try something different.

 Word from the Wise

"God wants you to be holy, so you should keep clear of all sexual sin. Then each of you will control your body and live in holiness and honor—not in lustful passion as the pagans do, in their ignorance of God and his ways." (1 Thessalonians 4:3,4)

Because Christian couples know God, their passion is not lustful and their lovemaking is a holy act. So allow your passion for your spouse to be unbridled!

Oral sex is a gift to your spouse. It is a gracious self-sacrificing gift. It tells your spouse that you are making their total pleasure your complete priority. You make sex all about their pleasure, not your own. For this reason, oral sex needs to be something a couple shares, not something only one spouse does for the other. To receive and not give it isn't quite fair. Perhaps you have that arrangement with your spouse, but is it fair? Is there some emotional reason your spouse can't give you oral sex? Women who have been sexually abused, where oral sex was the first abuse against them, won't be able to engage in oral sex of their own free choice until they have successfully completed therapy with a professional and their sexuality is completely healed and restored.

The best way to receive oral sex is when you don't ask for it. When the decision comes from your spouse because it's something they want to do for you. It's one thing to let your spouse know that you like or enjoy oral sex or to give them tips when they ask how you'd like it; it's quite another to expect it or demand it from your spouse. This sets up your relationship to experience frustration, disappointment, rejection, and possibly anger. What makes oral sex great is when your spouse is really into it because they really want to turn you on and they do it on their own volition.

Mutual Masturbation

This is another alternative to full-blown sex but is an integral part of lovemaking (see more at the end of Chapter 10). Simultaneously touching each other's genitals is a very normal part of sexual foreplay. In many ways it's almost required. For the woman, the arousal from being masturbated allows the vagina to become lubricated and relaxed in preparation for intercourse. For the man, the initial stimulation helps to ensure a fully erect penis. As a man ages, more and longer stimulation at this stage may be required. There are three ingredients for both husband and wife to have pleasurable touching of each other's genitals: warmth, moisture, and gentle pressure.

Manual Stimulation of Your Husband's Penis

Where does a woman learn how to satisfy her man through intensive attention to his penis? It sounds like something out of a porn flick. Well, it's not. What makes lovemaking something you want to come back to over and over is all in the quality of foreplay, not in the moment of orgasm. Yes, a man's penis is at the center of his manhood. For you to cherish his penis, enjoy his penis, and take care with his penis is very important to him. Wash your hands, trim you nails, take off your rings and watch, and "be there" emotionally, in addition to physically. What really turns your husband on is when you are "all there," with him, enjoying him. Here is how you will please your husband through manual stimulation. Have your husband sit up slightly with pillows supporting his back and head so that he can watch you (you can also have him sit on a chair or on the stairs with his legs spread). Sit between his legs. His penis needs to be at least semi-erect to start.

Back hand. Grasp the base of his penis with your hand in such a way that the backs of your hands are facing you, your thumb is at the bottom, pinky finger at the top, thumbs wrapped around the base of the penis. Move your hand up to the glans of the penis. When the heel of your hand reaches the top of the glans gently twist the head of the penis a quarter turn. Next, allow the palm of the hand to cup the top of the penis and gently twist another quarter turn. Now allow the glans to come up between your thumb and forefinger so that your knuckles are facing him and your thumb is now facing you and gently twist another quarter turn. Open up your hand and rub down the shaft of the penis so that your thumb is now on top, pinky finger at the bottom. Firmly slide your hand down his penis. Then start with the other hand. Keep alternating hands. You can use a little lubricant on your hands.

Cupped glans. Put a little lubricant in the palm of your hand. Grasp the head of the penis, the glans, with the palm of your hand and twist gently a little to the left and then a little to the right. Alternate hands so they don't get too tired too fast.

Two-hand clasp. Lubricate both of your hands. Grasp his penis with both hands allowing your fingers to interlock with each other and one thumb over the other. Your knuckles are facing him, your thumbs are facing you. Clasp only the shaft of his penis. Be snug, you are simulating a tight vagina. Pump both hands up and down the shaft of the penis in slow rhythmic motions. As you go up the shaft each time gently twist your hands in one direction or the other. Twist one direction as you go up and return to the original position on the way down. Think of how a washing machine twists and returns to its original position. Long, slow, twist, gentle, steady.

Pulsating two-hand clasp. Use the two-hand clasp, don't twist, but when you get to the top of the shaft simulate the pulsating motion of the vagina when it is contracting once each second during orgasm. As you pump him up and down squeeze your hands together to create a regulated pulsating motion. If he begins to ejaculate, stop pumping him and just hold him until he is done. His penis becomes very sensitive when he is ejaculating and pumping him at this point can be very irritating to him. As he is finishing ejaculating you can run your thumbs up his urethra to help him clean out his ejaculate.

One-handed stroking. Some men find it stimulating to have their testicles gently scratched or their inner thighs gently scratched while their penis is being stimulated. Using one hand to grasp his penis, thumb down, pinky on top with thumb wrapped around the bottom of his penis, rub him up and down, stopping just below the glans. Another alternative is to use a flat hand with all of your fingers held together to rub against the underside of his penis. While one hand is stimulating his penis, use the other hand to play with his testicles or his thighs, scratching gently. Another option for your free hand is to place it with your palm open just under his belly button and make slow stroking motions toward his penis.

Under the testicles. Lubricate your hand and spread your thumb apart from your four fingers. Cup your husband under his testicles. Slowly and gently rub up his testicles and continue up the shaft of the penis. Allow the testicles to gently slip back into place after you pass them. After you pass them allow your hand to grasp the penis firmly. Bring your hand back down again and over the testicles and start again. Keep contact with his penis at all times or it will break his focus in the pleasure you are giving him.

Umbrella. Lubricate your hands. Hold the base of his penis with one hand. Place your second hand over the glans. While gently stroking up and down the shaft of his penis with one hand, gently cup the glans and twist gently back and forth.

Horizontal vertical clasp. Clasp his penis with your left hand with your thumb up and pinky closest to his body. Your knuckles should be facing him and your thumb facing you. With your right hand, hold your fingers together with the tips of your fingers toward the glans and the heel of your hand at the base of his penis. Let the hand that is clasping the penis also grasp your flattened hand. Your flattened hand has the palm of your hand covering the length of his penis and your knuckles are facing you. Pump him up and down the shaft of his penis. As your flattened palm reaches the glans, let your index finger separate from the middle finger so that they come up under the ridge of the head of the penis.

When the webbed skin between these two fingers touches the ridge of the glans, let the fingers open to form a "V," then begin to point downward and push the webbing between your fingers down the shaft of his penis. Repeat over and over. From this position and with some of the others, when your thumbs are facing you use your thumbs to stimulate the underside of the shaft of his penis up to the glans. You can make circular motions with each thumb alternatively as they work their way up the shaft.

From the back. You can sit behind him and wrap your legs around him, breasts against his back, having as much skin to skin contact as possible and then masturbate him.

Ask him to teach you. Your husband may have found a way to masturbate himself that he finds the most satisfying. Ask him to teach you how he likes it. Have him place your hands under his so that he can show you the type of motion he likes and the amount of pressure he enjoys.

Breast rub. Lubricate your breasts, cup his penis between them and use them to stimulate him. Move your entire body up and down against him. You can also cup his penis between your breasts while twisting the glans with one hand. Go all the way down the shaft with your breasts and then breathe warm air on his glans when your mouth passes over. Kissing his penis will also be welcomed.

Jar opener. Clasp his penis with both hands, one above the other. Gently twist your hands in opposite directions and back again (like the washing machine). Both of your thumbs should be facing toward you and all of your knuckles should be facing him. When your top hand reaches the glans, cover it over with your hand, give a gentle twist, and then go down the shaft. Keep your hands touching. When your hands get to the base of the penis, let them come all the way down so that they both spread out over his pubic hair. Massage his pubic area gently and then begin your upward stoke. This is a good technique to use along with oral sex. Instead of having your top hand cover over his glans on the upward stroke, keep the tip of his penis in your warm moist mouth.

Hair and there. If you have long hair, wrap some of your hair around his penis, then grasp with both hands and pump him. This is a new and pleasurable sensation for him.

Pencil twirl. Have you ever put a pencil between your hands and rubbed your hands in opposite directions to make the pencil twirl? Try this with the shaft of his penis. Be gentle but quickly twirl back and forth on the shaft. Avoid the glans.

Tenting. Place the palms of your hands together. Open up the bottom of the palms of your hands and allow his penis to slide in. Remember to lubricate. Squeeze your hands firmly together around him, cross your thumbs, and pump up and down. Once you have trapped his penis between your hands, don't allow your hands to rub up and down on his skin. Squeeze firmly and only allow what motion his skin will allow. An optional position for your hands in this position is to allow the penis to slide up between the thumbs and index fingers with your fingers pointing toward his body instead of up toward the ceiling. Keep your thumbs crossed over each other. Pump him up and down from this position. Since the glans are not clasped you can move your hands up and down the shaft of his penis.

Patting and tapping. Some men like to have their penis tapped against the palm of your hand. Put a little lubricant in the palm of the receiving hand. Use the other hand to gently tap the penis into the receiving hand.

Finger circles. Lubricate your hands. Make a circle with your thumb and index finger on both hands. Slip your finger circles over his glans and move them up and down his penis while twisting the circles in opposite directions.

Manual Stimulation of Your Wife's Clitoris and Vagina

Women can have clitoral or vaginal orgasms or both. This tells you that both are highly sensitive. There are two parts to your wife's clitoris, the head and the glands. The head is like a little bulb and there are two glands that stem down from the head. Sometimes during stimulation or orgasm the head becomes so sensitive to touch that it can be painful. When this happens, your stimulation should move to the glands for continued pleasure.

Women can bring themselves to full orgasm in under two minutes, but it is much more pleasurable for them to spend an extended period of time being stimulated in multiple ways by and with their husbands.

Two-handed stimulation. When only hands are used, two-handed masturbation brings the most pleasure.

For two-handed stimulation use one hand (set of fingers) to gently massage the clitoris, while the other hand he can be providing touch and stimulation to the entire vulva, specifically, the labia minora (first inch and a half into the vagina).

It is sometimes hard to locate the clitoris. If you are new to marriage and sex you may need to first find it with the light on. Your wife may have to show it to you. You can waste many nights fumbling around trying to find it on your own or you can use her help (if she knows where it is). Sometimes both spouses are so sexually inexperienced (first time married virgins) that these are real questions because you really don't know. It's not your fault. It's something to rejoice about. But there can be too many wasted years spent trying to figure it all out on your own. While exploring your mate is intriguing and like being on a great quest, it's books like this that can help you make your explorations pay off in a big way!

Touching the clitoris is best done with your middle finger because it is larger than the others. Keep your fingernails trimmed short or you'll hurt your wife! Move your finger around until you can get the head of the clitoris under your finger. From there you can massage it in circular motions. You will notice that her clitoris becomes erect. However, it can also draw itself deeper into her body. You can lose it now and then and have to search for it a little.

One-handed stimulation. Holding your middle three fingers together you can rub her clitoris up and down. If your wrist is over her pubic hair and your fingers are pointing to her vagina this will work well. You can press your three fingers down through her vaginal opening (keeping the fingers on the outside) and rub her clitoris with the bones at the base of your middle finger. This is a one handed technique that stimulates both her clitoris and her vulva at the same time. There are three techniques known to please: (1) pressing the hand firmly against her and rubbing back and forth as if toward the back and then toward the belly, (2) side to side rubbing, and (3) patting up and down, pressing the fingers slightly into her tissues and up again; never losing contact with her tissues can produce great stimulation and possibly orgasm.

You can do this most easily if you are sitting behind her and she is in front of you. You can both lean back slightly. If you are behind her you can use your second hand to massage her breasts or pinch her nipples at the same time. If you are lying beside her you can reach your other arm over her shoulder and down to her breasts. If you spread your hand you should be able to put your baby finger on one nipple and your thumb on the other nipple. Press into the nipples or jiggle them while you are massaging her clitoris and vulva with the other hand. This will give her maximum pleasure. If you are behind her and she likes you to lick in her ear or blow in her ear or nibble her on the back of the neck at the same time, do it. Touch as much of her body at the same time as possible.

Sometimes just tapping the head of the clitoris with one finger can be pleasurable for her.

Don't forget her perineum in all this. Gentle rubbing will also be appreciated.

Penile stimulation. God designed your penis to please your wife. When your penis is erect, rub it against her clitoris and the lips of the labia minora. This is a sweet, gentle pleasure for women. This can be done when the two of you are both on your sides facing each other with your wife's upper thigh over your hip; or, if you sit behind her, you can reach around her and down to her vagina. While one hand is working her G-spot, the other hand can be massaging her breasts, and you can be kissing the back of her neck.

Mutual Body Massage

Full body massage alone can get a woman fully excited for intercourse. For a man, full body massage can cause erection to begin. Have you ever been for a professional massage? If you have you know that they massage the balls of the feet, the arch of the feet, the heel, each and every toe! The same is true for the hands—they will massage the inner and outer surface of the palm of the hand, the ball of the thumb, and the full length of each and every finger.

In the massage studio it's relaxing; when your spouse does it, it's a turn-on. Massage the muscles below the knee, the thighs, buttocks muscles, all the back, shoulders, upper arms, forearms, base of the skull, head, face, chest, pectorals, and breasts. It might be helpful for both of you to go for a couple's massage just so that you can learn some of the means and techniques that the masseuse uses. As your spouse massages you, pay attention to what parts feel better than others, what massage technique feels the best, and so on.

Licking and Sucking

Sucking each other's fingers and toes can also be a real turn-on. Deep moist licking and deep breathing in and around the ears can be a total turn-on and raise a person's sexual tension. Licking the abdomen, the tender tissue at the front of the armpit, and behind the knees can also be sensuous.

Licking and sucking your wife's breasts can help her both get turned on to sex so that she begins to vaginally lubricate. That extra attention on the breasts can really help her move to orgasm. Keeping her breasts moistened can help her get maximum pleasure. Lick your fingers and rub them on her nipples regularly during sex play. Put a little sterile lubricant on her nipples and blow on them!

Kissing

Our lips have a kazillion nerve endings in them. They are highly sensitive! Too often couples let sensual kissing slip away from them once they start having intercourse. Kissing is seen in dating as the way to achieve the most intimacy (if you practiced good sexual boundaries before marriage) and now that you can go further you may have relegated kissing further down in your sexual play.

Lips on lips, tongue on tongue is highly sensual, always. You just have to make it so. Some women can orgasm from kissing alone without any vaginal stimulation at all. What kind of a kisser are you? Do you please your spouse with the way you kiss them? Everyone kisses differently. Your former boyfriend/girlfriend may have loved the way you kiss, your former spouse may have loved it, too, but your spouse now might find your kissing a turn off. What to do, what to do! Instead of criticizing your spouse, tell them, I like to be kissed like this—and then show them how you like it. You can also ask your spouse what it's like for them when you kiss them. They will probably exaggerate a bit but you'll learn what you're doing that turns them off. We want to get turned on together, right? Right!

A closed mouth kiss is not romantic, neither is a woodpecker tongue going in and out of your mouth—lose the pointy tongue. Let your tongues explore each other's mouths. Run your tongue along your spouse's upper and lower teeth, around their tongue, and around their inner and outer lips (French kissing). Sucking your spouse's lower lip can be a turn-on.

Moisture is a turn-on no matter where your lips take you on your spouse's body. Kissing earlobes, belly buttons, toes, fingers, nipples, back of the knees, base of the back of the neck, inner side of arm at the elbow joint, the small of the back, the eyelids, can all be a turn-on. If in doubt pay attention to the reaction you get or ask a simple question.

Eskimo kissing is the tender touching of noses and cheeks. This can be a fun, tender type of touching. Butterfly kisses are the gentle fluttering of your eyelashes on your lover; this can be sweet. Hickeys? They went out with high school—in case nobody told you!

Kissing is a before, during, and after activity of lovemaking. It's something you always come back to. Kisses can start the whole lovemaking time and can polish it off during the "afterglow."

Brush well, floss well, use mouthwash, make your mouth attractive to your spouse!

Firm, Direct Touching

Touching the breasts and penis during foreplay is usually best experienced when it is firm and direct. Don't fiddle with her breasts, take a good hold (unless she directs you differently), hold firmly, massage firmly (squeeze nipples gently). Take hold of his penis firmly—gentle fiddling won't do anything for him.

Putting on the Condom

Wives can help their husbands put on their condoms (if you use them) during foreplay. Your husband may prefer to do it himself but offer to do it for him.

You can either put it on him like he does it for himself or you can put the condom in your mouth, hold the tip of the condom with your lips, put your mouth on the tip of his penis, and push it down over his glans with your mouth. Push it as far down as you can push it and then, with your mouth still on the glans, push it down the rest of the length of the penis with your finger tips.

You can put a drop of sterile lubricant in the tip of the condom and on the top of his penis so that there is moisture inside the condom during the rest of the sex play and during intercourse. This will increase the sensitivity of the glans and make it more pleasurable for him.

Move quickly with the lubricant. You don't want it to run down his penis. This will cause the condom to slip off more easily.

Lipstick and lip-gloss can break down the latex condom, so make sure your lips have nothing on them when you do this. If you need a little lubrication, use a sterile water-based lubricant. Condoms can be broken down by all other types of lubricants. You don't need fancy "love shop" lubricants. The basic sterile lubricant from your local pharmacy is all you need. This is known as the Italian Method!

Regarding condoms: After ejaculation, make sure you grasp the bottom of the condom and hold it against you tightly as you withdraw your penis. Tie the condom to prevent the ejaculate from escaping and making a mess. Now and then it will happen that your penis might go soft or it might just slip off and get "lost" inside your wife. Condoms also break on occasion. Either you or she will have to reach into her vagina with your fingers and pull it out. Most couples will experience this at some time or another. This raises concern about contraception. Everyone who has had this experience knows condoms are not full proof birth control or STD prevention devices. They only work when they work.

Condoms are not only used for birth control. Sometimes it's nice for you to put on a condom and catch the ejaculate so that your wife can just go to sleep after the "afterglow" rather than have to get up and go to the bathroom for the ejaculate to drain. If she's super tired and is making love with you mostly as a favor to you, bless her by using a condom (whether you need one or not for contraception).

Lubricating

Women's bodies ebb and flow with their estrogen. When estrogen is low, vaginal lubrication is low. She can be dry right after she ovulates each month as a predictable event. Birth control pills can cause vaginal dryness. As she begins her peri-menopausal phase and her estrogen ebbs, she will also experience vaginal dryness.

Sterile lubricants will be a necessary part of comfortable sex both for the husband and the wife. Both husband and wife should have their bottle of sterile lubricant.

During foreplay, two things happen. As a woman is sexually turned on her vaginal area begins to lubricate itself, and when a woman's vaginal tissues are well lubricated she will be more turned on. Some women know that licking their fingers and making their vaginal tissues moist will hasten the coming of an orgasm.

If the wife is vaginally dry, reach up into her vagina and bring some of her own natural lubricant down (remember, the fluids start far up inside her vagina). You can also lick her with your tongue to moisten her, or lick your fingers and moisten her that way. She can also moisten herself through licking her fingers and rubbing them on her vulva, or either of you can moisten her with sterile lubricant.

Women will self-lubricate up until orgasm and then her fluids can dry up pretty quickly. You may have to add lubrication before his penis can penetrate with comfort. Your wife can pour some lubricant on her hands and rub your entire penis with the lubricant. Rubbing the lubricant in your hands before applying it to your spouse will warm it up. You can also pour a little lubricant in his belly button (if he's on his back) and tip his penis forward and rub it in the lubricant. If you're on top of him doing this will be an erotic experience for your husband. You can pour some lubricant on your fingers and gently massage her vulva with the lubricant, then, you're good to go. The application of lubricant to each other can be a very sensual activity to add to your sex play.

The Anus

Relying on the fact that you have both just showered and scrubbed, many couples enjoy it when their spouse licks the area around their anus. There are lots of nerve endings there and there is pleasure to be had.

The anus can also be stimulated with the fingertips or the heel of the hand through gentle pressure and a massaging motion. You can try massaging the anus with the heel of the hand while massaging the perineum with the index finger. Keep the motion going or the perineum could start feeling numbness.

While stimulating the anus and perineum with one hand you can also be stimulating your spouse's penis or clitoris and give them a mind-blowing experience.

The sphincter muscle in both men and women wraps around the anus and the penis/vagina, and in women only, the urethra. During orgasm this entire muscle contracts. Many people are not aware that the sphincter wrapping around the anus contracts during orgasm.

Keep in mind that any fingers that touch the anus should never then come anywhere near the vagina until they are washed with soap and water. You must protect the woman from potential infection!

Anal Sex

The only reference to anal sex in the Bible is in the context of homosexuality. The Bible is silent on this topic with regard to married couples. Anal intercourse is, like all other forms of sexual contact, to be at the discretion of the couple themselves. It must be something that both husband and wife want to try or do of their own volition. The thought of anal sex is repulsive to many people but not to all.

The vagina was designed by God to receive a penis; the anus wasn't. But for that matter, neither was the mouth! As such, the anus provides none of its own lubrication, so if you are going to have anal sex you must use lubrication. Some men like to use condoms also because of the bacteria in the anus.

One caution about anal sex: Since the anus was not created to receive a penis, it is possible to literally wear out the anal sphincter muscle. The vagina was created with an opening already wide enough for the penis to enter. The rectum and anus were made for a different purpose and function differently: When enough fecal matter builds up in the rectum, it puts pressure on the anal sphincter, causing it to relax, open and release the fecal matter. The anal sphincter was not built to stay open, but to open momentarily and quickly seal again. It is a physical reality that repeated anal intercourse can cause fecal incontinence. Once you've gotten to this point there is no going back. There are some creative surgical innovations that can help you, but who wants to have it go that far? If you are going to engage in anal sex, do it only rarely for variety. The consequences for your wife are irreversible. The anus can stretch to the point where it won't contract again and stay closed.

There can be negative consequences when we use parts of our bodies for purposes God did not intend. It's just a reality.

The Male G-Spot

The man's G-spot, like the woman's, is about two inches up into his body, just behind the pubic bone. The only way to stimulate it is through the anus. Because there is no lubrication in the anus, you'll need to lubricate if you try to stimulate him there. You could use a latex glove and lubricate the finger of the glove, as doctors do. You would reach up to your second knuckle joint. He'll really respond if you make contact with it.

The Female G-Spot

If your wife has discovered her G-spot, stimulate it with your middle finger. Slip it into the vagina up to about two inches. Use your hand to sort of cup her pubic bone. Your finger will then want to pull itself back as if trying to touch the middle of the palm of your hand. You'll be pressing your finger toward her pubic bone. The G-spot is only the size of a bean. Ask her to let you know when you've touched it. (Well, you may not have to ask—if you touch it, she'll respond.)

Kegel Exercises

We've mentioned sphincter muscles a few times. As stated, they are the figure 8 muscles that wrap around a woman's urethra, vagina, and anus and around a man's penis and anus. Every woman who has been in prenatal classes has learned Kegel exercises. It's unfortunate that most couples don't learn about them sooner than this. If our sphincter muscles get out of shape we can leak urine and feces. Yuck! This is preventable through Kegel exercises, which are designed specifically to keep these muscles in shape.

An added bonus of strengthening our sphincter muscles is the fact that they wrap around the vagina. With toned up sphincter muscles a woman can squeeze her husband's penis and playfully trap it inside her (but she can't actually keep her husband from withdrawing his penis). A tighter vagina can give both spouses more pleasure. Since the first inch and a half of the vagina (labia minora) is highly sensitive, and considering a woman can get an orgasm through stimulation of the labia minora alone, with well toned sphincters a woman can increase the likelihood of having a vaginal orgasm during vaginal intercourse.

How do you do a Kegel exercise? The next time you go to the bathroom, try to stop your urine flow midstream. Those are your sphincter muscles pulling together to try to shut off the plumbing. (Do this only to detect your sphincter muscle. Stopping the flow of your urine can cause you urinary problems.) Once the sphincter muscles are engaged, the entire figure 8 muscle contracts together. Now that you know what it is like to contract the sphincter you will want to practice contracting it while you aren't urinating. Pregnant women are told to contract their sphincter for 10 seconds at a time before releasing and to do this 100 times per day. You may have to work up to 10 seconds, but keep working at it. We do resistance training to keep our other muscles toned; we need to do Kegel exercises to keep our "sexual muscles" toned.

One thing that every marital bed needs is an overhead ceiling fan. To have a cool breeze blowing while your bodies, minds, and souls are getting hot, hot, hot can help the two of you to enjoy your experience together all that much longer.

Word from the Wise

"Love each other with genuine affection and take delight in honoring each other. Never be lazy in your work, but serve the Lord enthusiastically." (Romans 12:10,11)

Romance is hard work, but don't cut corners. Your spouse can detect insincerity when you're only in a rush to have sex. This is really a form of laziness and isn't truly honoring your spouse.

Please keep in mind these are all ideas or suggestions. Your loved one and their comfort must be your top priority. Just because these ideas have been known to bring pleasure to some couples doesn't mean that you and your spouse will be adding them to your sexual menu.

If all this seems overwhelming to try to remember, don't worry! You don't have to remember everything or even try it all at once. Focus on two or three things that you feel comfortable trying. What you will discover as you and your spouse enjoy each other sexually is that certain touching and techniques will, indeed, come naturally.

In the next chapter, we'll take a look at a variety of positions for making love.

Chapter 10

Doing It: Part 2

There is a variety, although not endless, of positions for making love. All positions, as long as you and your spouse are both comfortable, are "good" positions. There is no biblically endorsed list of sexual positions. This is an area where the Bible is silent, which means that God has left it up to your imagination! If there's a position that you and your spouse want to try, then try it. If it works, great. If not, try another. In this chapter, we'll take a look at the transition from arousal to intercourse, including descriptions of a few basic positions.

Coming Together

Once arousal hits a peak during foreplay, it's time to come together and enjoy sexual intercourse. The right moment to make the shift will vary for every couple, and will even vary each time you make love. Sometime you'll want to get right to the bump and grind, and other times you'll want to linger in the foreplay stage. In fact, as suggested above, as something different, you may decide to go for orgasm without actually having intercourse. That's fine, too! Whether you share orgasm through mutual masturbation, oral sex, or vaginal intercourse doesn't matter. What matters is the loving encounter you share together.

The key is to ensure that both are ready to move on to vaginal penetration. Typically, but not always, men are in more of a hurry to just have sex than women are. However, when a wife learns great techniques to please her husband through manual stimulation or oral sex he won't be so anxious to get to vaginal penetration.

Be patient with each other and exercise give and take. Sometimes, your wife can agree to move right to intercourse, and at other times, the man can agree to lovingly extend foreplay as long as his wife wants. Sometimes it's the other way around—your wife may want to get straight to vaginal intercourse because she is totally horny and you aren't ready to go there yet. This is not really a male/female difference. Sometimes one person just gets into that intense sexual mode on their own from their thoughts, from sights or sounds and wants to get it on right now. The spouse that is hot to trot needs to wait! Quickies are fun, especially when you're young, newlyweds, and in a childless house—but they are not always possible.

A woman generally cannot be rushed into intercourse without the addition of lubricants. It takes time for her juices to start flowing, so if you're the one who is hot to trot first, slow down. Doing it too quickly and without lubrication can actually be painful for her. If she wants to get there quickly with you but is vaginally dry, use a sterile lubricant. Guys, sometimes you just have to chill!

You have to both be ready to come together. Don't rush each other.

For Him

There are enough ideas in this chapter to put a lot of spice into any couple's sex life. Keep in mind that a great sex life develops over years. This chapter might leave you wanting your wife to try all this stuff all at once. She might be totally overwhelmed by what she's read here. Give her time, don't push, let her try these things as she is ready.

The woman, if she is waiting to orgasm through intercourse, needs to know that fewer than 30 percent of women orgasm with vaginal intercourse alone. If you want to orgasm together, most likely, your wife will also have to have her clitoris stimulated at the same time (either by you or her). You'll be given some ideas to make this happen. More often than not, vaginal intercourse won't bring your wife to orgasm. This is why you need to learn to please her apart from vaginal intercourse.

Wives, know this: Your husband wants you to orgasm. He just needs to know how to do it for you. Men take pleasure in their ability to please their wives and drive them wild sexually. He'll be really pleased with himself when he can help you have two or three or four orgasms in a single lovemaking encounter!

Positions

Here are descriptions of the basic positions upon which all others are pretty much based. Again, the key is to be sensitive to each other, experiment gently and carefully, and to not force the other into a position he or she is not comfortable with.

Man on Top

Commonly referred to as the missionary position, this is also the most commonly known arrangement of bodies for lovemaking. This is usually what is portrayed in the movies. This position allows the man the most freedom of movement for thrusting.

The woman lies flat on her back with her legs spread open to receive her husband. The woman may position herself three different ways in response to her husband: (1) she might wrap her legs around his back, (2) she might lift her legs up so that her feet lay on his shoulders, or (3) she could have her knees raised up.

The husband positions himself between the woman's legs. He may hold himself up with his hands flat and arms outstretched, or he may rest on his elbows, or he may lie directly on top of his wife. He may have one arm around the back of her neck and the other around her waist, or may even grasp her buttocks with his hands (women like to have their hips and butts grasped during intercourse). The man needs to be sensitive to how much pressure he is putting on his wife in this position, and may want to position his torso a little to one side rather than directly on her.

If the husband has a protruding belly, that belly can push your wife's insides up into her chest and compress her lungs. She might be gasping for air. Also, depending on how long each of your torsos are, your upper chest might press on her throat if you lay right on top of her. She will have problems breathing like this also. You may still be able to lie on top of her if you prop up one of your shoulders and relieve her of the pressure of your body. Hint: Get on the treadmill! Women like to have their husbands lying on them, having their buttocks clasped, and so on. Your protruding belly is not healthy for you and without it, you could provide her more enjoyment of the touch of your body. Instead of focusing on breathing she'll be free to focus on how good you feel!

For your wife, this might be the preferred position because it can give her the most body contact with you. To feel you lay on her chest, on her breasts can feel very good to her sexually and emotionally. When a man is in this position with his wife with full out body contact and they are hugging and kissing at the same time, she has a sense of safety and security with her man.

While your husband is on top, clutch his buttocks, run your hands up and down his back with gentle massage, grab him behind his thighs and help him thrust himself into you, run your fingers through his hair, and kiss his face.

If this position isn't all that sexually stimulating for the wife, your options are as follows: (1) the husband can do this position on his knees and use one hand to stimulate her clitoris (this isn't that easy for a man); (2) the wife can slip her hand down to her clitoris and stimulate it while he is thrusting (options 1 and 2 can allow you to both orgasm together); (3) the husband, with penis in her vagina, can try to gently rock his pelvis bone up and down against her clitoris with about a two inch range of motion (continuous motion like this might bring her to orgasm in this position; you may have to spread the lips of the labia majora a bit to expose the clitoris and make it more accessible to be rubbed by the pubic bone).

Remember, for a woman, the greatest orgasmic pleasure is to have something touching her vulva, her clitoris, and breasts at the same time. If your husband is resting on his hands in this position you can grab your own breasts and rub them with one hand while using the other hand to stimulate your clitoris. Lick your fingers and wet your nipples and this will help you orgasm with him in this position.

Woman on Top

This one is great for making her do all the work! The man lies flat on his back and the woman straddles him facing him. She may sit upright on her knees or lay on top of the man's chest with her legs straddled outside of his, turning her pelvis up to better hold his penis inside her vagina. The man can leave his legs flat or raise his knees, whichever is most comfortable for him. The wife needs to raise and lower herself over her husband's penis, paying attention to keep a steady rhythmic pace. Ask him if he wants it faster or slower.

One real advantage of this position is that a woman can have her husband's penis in her (something touching her vulva) and at the same time, she can open up her labia majora and make her clitoris rub against her husband's pubic bone. Women need to be careful when they do this. It feels good to rub hard but you can also tear tissue in your clitoral area and you could end up with blood in your urine or with a bladder infection (pee after you're done to clear the urethra of possible bacteria).

If your wife is on top she will pretty much do all the work. She can kiss your face, suck your lips, massage your chest, reach behind her and massage your inner thighs, and lick your nipples.

You can't be totally receiving though. As she is coddling your penis in her vagina, you could rub her face, rub your hands through her hair, lick her ears or breathe in them if she lies down on her chest. If she is resting on her wrists or sitting on you, grab hold of both of her breasts and massage them. You may also reach down to her clitoris and stimulate it while she is moving herself up and down on top of you.

Most of the time your husband will be able to orgasm in this position, but not always. This position may be great for you but not enough for him.

Wife on Top Facing Backward

An alternative is for the woman to straddle the man with her back to him, facing his feet. It is in this position that the penis is rubbing more directly into the front of the vagina up against the pubic bone. The woman thrusts forward and back the way a swing moves. One thing that a woman can enjoy through this position is the stimulation of her G-spot. Continuous stimulation of the G-spot can produce orgasm. The G-spot is a spot about 2 inches into the vagina behind the pubic bone and is about the size of a bean. Not all women are aware of this spot, and some don't have it. To find out if you have a sensitive G-spot you can either probe into your vagina yourself or ask your husband to do it.

Man Entering from Behind

With the wife on her elbows and knees the husband enters from the rear. A double pillow for her to rest her head on should be set up. This is the other position where your husband's penis will hit your G-spot. From this position a man can have his penis in his wife's vagina while he uses one hand to stimulate her clitoris and the other to massage her breasts. Or he might massage her breasts with both hands. In this position it is easy for a woman to rock back and forth while her husband thrusts into her. Holding onto your wife's hips is also nice for her and helps you keep positioned with her vagina. This position can also be accomplished with the wife lying flat on her belly or she can be standing and bent over.

On the Side

There are a couple of basic variations to this position.

Facing each other: The couple lay on their sides layering their legs. This position doesn't offer a lot of stimulation for the wife. One of you will need to manually stimulate her clitoris if you want to orgasm together. This position is nice because you can enjoy kissing each other during intercourse. You can also massage and stroke each other's backs. Your husband can massage your breasts with his hand. You can also reach to each other's buttocks and thighs to pull each other closer.

Man behind his wife: The man faces the woman, who has her back to him, and enters her vagina from behind. This is a very comfortable position requiring less exertion than the others. It also allows for deep penetration by the man. Some men report that the back entry position gives them the greatest sexual pleasure in vaginal intercourse. When the man is in this position if the woman lifts her upper leg her husband can reach through and stimulate her clitoris during intercourse. He may be able to reach across the top of his wife's thigh to the clitoris and if she turns slightly back toward him kissing is possible, also.

With this variation he can often extend his lower arm under her head and down to her breast and provide full stimulation for her (breast, clitoris, and vulva all at once). Also, he can rub her back, hold on to her shoulders, or reach forward to play with her breasts. In this position it may be difficult for women to orgasm so either he can reach through to stimulate your clitoris or you can reach down, lift your upper leg slightly and stimulate yourself to orgasm with him as he is thrusting. This is a good position for a pregnant woman.

Sitting or Kneeling

One variation is where the man sits and the woman straddles his lap. If she is facing him he can suck his wife's breasts and you can kiss easily. She can also sit with her back to his chest or sit on his lap facing sideways. The husband may have to work to move you up and down over his penis or you will have to extend your arms down and push yourself up and down. It sort of depends on your body sizes. This position doesn't allow for a great deal of motion.

A woman can sit on the edge of the bed and her husband can kneel forward and penetrate her vagina although it's harder for him to move. If he is sitting on a chair with arms it will be easier for you to brace yourself to move up and down on him. Also, if the wife lays on her back and pulls her knees up to her chest on the edge of the bed, her husband can, from a standing position, lean forward and thrust into her. If she spreads her legs slightly he can stimulate her clitoris at the same time.

If the woman is sitting facing her husband during vaginal intercourse it is easy for her to hug him and rub his back, run her hands through his hair, kiss him, and so on. It is also easier for her to stimulate herself and bring herself to orgasm with him.

The last sitting position is one in which the couple sits facing each other with legs fully extended on the bed. The wife should be sitting slightly on her husband. Her legs will be spread so it will be easy for her husband to stimulate her clitoris while his penis is inside of her. From this position it is easy for the woman to bring her legs around and underneath her and move into a position of being on top of him. He need simply lie down from here.

Standing

Yes, it's possible to have sex standing up. Usually you'll want to lean against a wall or something secure to keep from falling over! It can be done face to face, or in a rear entry position where the woman leans over a table as the man enters her from behind. If you are both standing he can lower himself to get into you or he can lift you up onto his hips so that you can straddle him. He will then take hold of your buttocks and maneuver the thrusting.

The standing position is best suited for a short, intense sexual experience together. It doesn't lend itself to the long slow build of the man-on-top or woman-on-top positions.

From any position a wife can contract her sphincter muscles while her husband's penis is inside her. When she is tighter it is nicer for him. This may also squeeze her husband's penis against her G-spot, increasing her pleasure simultaneously.

From these basic positions all other positions develop. Use your imagination and see how many combinations you and your spouse can come up with that fit your comfort level, and your physical abilities.

For Her

Believe it or not there are rare occurrences of a woman being allergic to her husband's semen. If you end up with vaginal irritation after intercourse you should see an allergy specialist. The doctor can give you two to three shots of immunotherapy (with some of your husband's sperm used to make to potion) and your body will develop a tolerance for his sperm.

After a man has climaxed he knows he's totally out of steam. This is not necessarily true for women. If she is still desirous of another orgasm you can gently stimulate her to orgasm as you lay beside her or the two of you can just enjoy the afterglow together. If the husband orgasms before his wife, he needs to continue to stimulate her to bring her to orgasm before he can relax and enter into afterglow with her.

Positions for Oral Sex

When it comes to oral sex, any position that's comfortable and allows the mouth and genitals to meet will work! A common position is called sixty-nine. Why? Because the number 69 suggests the position a husband and wife take to enjoy mutual oral sex.

A Few Cautions

It is possible for a man to fracture his penis. This is very rare but it can happen if his penis slams into her pubic bone. If this should happen he needs to immediately get to the emergency room at the nearest hospital so that repair work can begin.

If she experiences pain during deep intercourse, your penis may be bumping up against her cervix. Try another position.

If a woman is on top of her husband during vaginal intercourse and lays totally backward, his penis may be able to tolerate it but maybe not. Go easy and if he indicates you shouldn't do that, don't try it again.

When a woman is on top and rubbing her clitoris against his pubic bone, she needs to be careful how forcefully she bumps or rubs against him. It's easy to tear tissue this way.

Any time your spouse is physically or emotionally uncomfortable or uneasy, you need to slow down, back off, and perhaps avoid the type of activity you were just doing.

Dr. Truth

Each of you is totally responsible to communicate your sexual needs and desires to your spouse. Each of you must take responsibility to teach your spouse through telling or showing them, what works for you sexually. Let your spouse know your sexual preferences or what you'd like to try. Then, leave it there. After this, focus on pleasing your mate and being totally there and present during lovemaking. What you have told your mate will stay in their minds and over time they will make decisions to please you the way you want to be pleased.

Masturbation

Were you taught that masturbation was a forbidden word? Certainly, it doesn't sound like a very nice word. Too bad they couldn't have come up with a better one than that!

There are parts of the Christian church that teach masturbation is a sin. Let's clarify. Masturbation can be a sin, but is not a sin in and of itself. What makes masturbation a sin? (I'm referring here to masturbation that you do alone, not mutual touching with your spouse during lovemaking.)

C. S. Lewis wrote an essay on masturbation some time ago and basically taught that masturbation is a sin because it makes one a god unto oneself.

Masturbation is sin if it includes lust. Masturbation is a sin if, while masturbating, you fantasize about someone who is not your spouse *or* if you fantasize about your spouse doing things with you that they would never agree do to in real life.

We know that when we do something in our mind, in the eyes of the Lord, we have done it in real life.

For women it is possible to masturbate without having anyone in mind at all. It is possible to masturbate for the sheer pleasure of it. It generally takes women 1½ to 2 minutes to achieve orgasm when they stimulate themselves.

A Franciscan Father, teaching at Fuller Theological Seminary, gave a talk about where lust and sin began. He said that when he first sees an attractive woman, he has a natural, immediate, physiological response to what he sees and that response is one of sexual attraction/stimulation. This is a natural human response to attractive stimuli. This is not sin. Where sin could enter in, is if he allowed that initial thought to stay and began to put sexual thoughts with it—sexual thoughts of him doing things with the woman. At this point, he pointed out, he is making her do something in his mind that she would not choose to do. In this moment, he is violating her will. This is the sin.

It is the violation of another human being's will during lust that makes lust a sin. You can victimize a person's soul without them knowing it. Whether or not they know it does not determine its sinfulness.

Can you lust after your own spouse? Yes. Lust begins in your imagination the moment that you fantasize doing anything with your spouse that they find repulsive, offensive, morally wrong, or the like. When you fantasize about them doing in your mind what they would never agree to do in real life, you are lusting after them and it is sin, even if it is your spouse. It's all about violation of the will, whether in your mind or in real life.

How else can masturbation be sin?

When masturbation is excessive and becomes a controlling force in one's life.

What does that mean?

When masturbation becomes the focus of your day so that you find yourself planning your day around opportunities to masturbate, you have a problem (whether you are fantasizing about another person or not). You would be well advised to get counseling if this is true for you.

One thing that has been observed is the high correlation between masturbation and emotional well-being. Those who are found to excessively masturbate often have more emotional and social problems than those for whom masturbation is not an issue.

How else can masturbation be sin?

When it replaces relationship with other human beings or is used to avoid intimacy with our spouse, then it is sin.

What place does masturbation have in a marriage?

During times of sickness, marital difficulties, personal grief or trauma, military assignments, and so on, lovemaking may wane or be completely impossible. Sexual tension still builds within people and both spouses need to deal with it. It's a good idea for couples to talk about this and make agreements about it during times of marital peace. A couple may agree together that masturbation is an option for each of them during these times. The idea of solo masturbation may be offensive to the couple and they may try to do other things to distract them from their body's need for sexual release. If they choose this option, their bodies will find sexual release at night when they sleep.

 Word from the Wise

"You have heard that the law of Moses says, 'Do not commit adultery.' But I say, anyone who even looks at a woman with lust in his eye has already committed adultery with her in his heart.'" (Matthew 5:27-28)

Having sexual desire for your spouse (whether experienced in mind, emotions, or body) is legitimate. But the Bible calls it "lust" when these feelings are directed toward anyone else, and the word is equated only with sin. Keep your mind on your spouse and keep your soul pure before God.

Improving It

Great sex involves more than fantastic foreplay followed by the perfect position and earth-moving orgasms. There are a few other things to consider that can further enhance your sexual pleasure and satisfaction.

Timing

When it comes to opening a business, they say the three keys to success are location, location, location! In sex, you could say, there are also three keys to success: timing, timing, and timing!

There's the timing of when to have sex, how to have sex, and having sex.

Timing when to have sex will depend on whether you're trying to get pregnant, what your mutual schedules are like, where the kids are, and other factors. For young, healthy newlyweds who aren't consumed with their careers, just about any time (and place!) they're together seems right. Scheduling isn't much of an issue unless the two are workaholics, work conflicting schedules or work out of town and come home exhausted.

When getting pregnant becomes an issue, then timing sex when your wife is most likely to conceive can be critical. As you both age and your family expands, your general health and physical stamina, having kids in the house, and more will have an increasing impact on the best timing for sex.

The timing of how to have sex requires knowing when to talk about sex. Not every time will be a good time to have sex or to talk about having sex. Generally, any discussion you have about your married sex life needs to take place in private, well away from prying ears. Depending on the sensitivity of the specific topic, you'll also need to consider your spouse's receptiveness.

Discussing some aspect of what's happening or not happening in your bedroom while at a family reunion is not a good idea.

Bringing up a sexual issue just as you are about to have sex is not necessarily a good thing. Unless it's a comment directly related to what's happening, such as please do what you're doing faster, slower, or with less pressure, bringing up an issue can put a damper on the situation. While you're having sex, focus on the sex you're having.

Maybe after you're done and enjoying the afterglow and you're cuddling together, this may be a time to gently raise a concern or an idea. Sometimes it's better to talk about things you'd like to adjust in your sexual activities the next day when there is no plan to have sex so egos and emotions might not be as sensitive.

Whenever you choose to discuss something as delicate as sex with your spouse, be kind, gentle, and respectful, and do it in private when there's no chance of anyone, especially kids, overhearing or walking into the middle of your discussion.

It's a delicate subject that can hurt feelings and it would also be a good idea to pray that God will join together your hearts and minds before you talk.

Finally there's the timing of what you're doing when you're doing it! Timing affects men in that younger men can usually get to orgasm quickly. As a man ages, achieving orgasm can take longer. The same can be true for women. At any age, how long it takes you to become aroused, ready for sex, and reaching orgasm can be affected by your mood, your health, distractions nearby (like the phone ringing or something noisy going on outside), and other factors.

Don't expect that every time you and your spouse make love that everything will always happen on the same timeline. There are times when you'll want to proceed more slowly and delay orgasm. Sometimes orgasm will delay itself, while at other times you may both be surprised at how quickly it comes. Learn to read each other's bodies and responses to learn how to time foreplay and intercourse to better fulfill each other's desires.

Illness, injury, and pregnancy can all make sex wait.

Word from the Wise

"There is a time for everything, a season for every activity under heaven." (Ecclesiastes 3:1)

Yes, there are even times and seasons for sex. There are ebbs and flows to every relationship. During difficult times sex may be less frequent. It's during times of sexual abstinence when a couple can deepen their physical and emotional intimacy without intercourse.

Talking

Once you've determined a good time for talking, each spouse should feel comfortable bringing up sexual issues. Men tend to be more reluctant to enter into discussions about sex; some people are just shy. Be gentle, kind, and patient when raising the issue. Sometimes it is best for wives just to mention to their husbands what some of their sexual preferences are, thank him for listening and let the subject go. He truly may not know how to respond to you. Don't force responses but allow him to listen and then think about what you have to say. Some issues may require some thinking time. That's fine. Give them space.

Never let a huge issue related to sex or any other part of your marriage go unresolved. Not talking about it will only wear you down and make you miserable, which will affect your spouse's mood. If it's hard to talk about, perhaps you both need to go to counseling. You pastor may be helpful. Or you may want to go alone to learn some strategies for bringing the topic up with your spouse.

Talking during sex can also be good, or it can be a turn-off. Some couples enjoy talking a bit graphically to each other while making love. This is fine as long as the language is not obscene or demeaning. There are plenty of ways to express a whole range of sexual thoughts with your spouse without resorting to crude and obscene language.

Any talking should be done only if comfortable for both. For some, talking, no matter what the words being spoken, can be such a distraction that they're unable to stay aroused. For some couples, talking about the kinds of sexual involvement they would like with each other is a real turn-on. Before you talk during sex, you probably should talk about talking well before or sometime after sex.

Agree as to whether or not talking is okay, what words and topics are acceptable and not acceptable, and how much talking should occur.

> **For Him**
>
> If you want to have a long and happy life with your wife, you probably want to avoid teasing her in any way about her appearance or weight. Any teasing you do should be light and not critical. If she doesn't take it that way, don't do it again. Keep in mind that women often like to be told that you find them sexy no matter what size or shape they are. They don't care if they are attractive to every man in the world, only you!

Teasing

Everyone teases and hates to be teased! We first encounter teasing as children. In most instances it's harmless, but it can sometimes be harsh. Children can be especially harsh with other children, making fun of someone who's a little different (tall, short, skinny, fat, or whatever). With our families and close friends, the teasing that usually occurs is harmless and even a form of affection. It's playful and light, and can even affirm our acceptance with one another.

In marriage, teasing is an area to tread carefully. Coming from different backgrounds can guarantee a slight difference in what is viewed as acceptable or unacceptable teasing.

Generally, err on the side of caution if you tease your spouse. Aim to be as inoffensive as possible. Pay attention to the response you get. If there's any sign of hurt feelings, explain that you were only teasing. If there are areas your spouse says are off limits to teasing, respect those limits.

Over time, you and your spouse can develop playful ways of teasing each other that will be fun and can even be the start of a lovemaking session. However, never tease about what occurs sexually between you. Some topics are inappropriate as topics of teasing. This type of teasing is really a form of making fun of your spouse and should be avoided.

Of course, there is sexual teasing that can occur between spouses that is a little turn-on for both of you and that you can share in passing throughout the day. This kind of teasing is part of sex play even though you are nowhere near the bedroom.

Calling your spouse on the phone at work and letting them know that the bed will be warm when they get home tonight is a little tease. Make sure your spouse doesn't mind this. When your wife is cooking dinner, coming up behind her and nibbling on her ear and letting her know how sexy she is also is sexual teasing. It's playing with each other, creating a little bit of fun with each other. She may also enjoy your coming up from behind and gently squeezing her breasts or her buttocks. If she's offended by this, don't do it. If in doubt, ask her.

What kind of sexual teasing play would you like your husband or wife to do toward you? Tell them. Then, one day, they'll probably surprise you by doing some of the stuff you've told them you'll like.

For Her

It's easy to make the mistake of thinking that men don't feel emotion as deeply as women. This is not necessarily true. Men are just as sensitive as women about certain issues. If your teasing yields a negative response from your husband, pay attention! You've probably touched on a topic that you don't want to tease him about.

Having Fun

Sex is fun in and of itself. At least it should be! Sex with your spouse is kind of like a roller coaster ride. Think about it. You both decide to go on a "ride" and the anticipation builds. The more you think about it, the more excited you become. It can also be a little scary. As you approach the ride, you hold hands and cling to each other. Once in your seats, the coaster moves slowly up the incline toward the first drop and your excitement builds. You reach the top and whoosh down you go! There are turns and loops, fast rushes and slower moments. When the ride is over, it takes time for the excitement to fade and your heart to stop racing as you both giggle over the exhilaration you have just experienced.

Yes, it's okay to laugh and experience emotional joy during sex! If there are no kids around, you might want to be more verbal in your expressions of how much fun you're having. Your verbalizations don't necessarily have to be real words. Sex can be a little more fun when you get to add in the sound effects. Of course, when kids are down the hall you have to be quiet—that's why you have to get them all out of the house now and then.

Sex should be similar. As you grow older, the roller coaster may be more like a Ferris wheel, but that's okay. Ferris wheels are fun, too!

Fun needs to happen outside the bedroom, too. Watching movies, going for walks, playing board games together, skiing, roller blading, and any number of activities from the sedate to the extreme are open to you to enjoy as a couple. What you choose to do for fun is up to you. Everyone's personalities are a little different. What's a hoot for one person is a snooze for another. You will both have different ideas about fun, but odds are you can find at least a couple of things you can agree on.

Fun is also a state of mind (kind of like sex!). Maintaining a sense of humor about life and being able to laugh at yourself will contribute toward your having fun together.

By the way, letting yourself have fun during sex includes not being self conscious about your natural facial expressions. Sometimes women feel self conscious about the facial expressions and grimaces they make during intense sexual stimulation. Don't hide yourself from your husband; your expressions are totally normal and can be a real turn-on for him.

> ### Word from the Wise
>
> "A cheerful heart is good medicine." (Proverbs 17:22)
>
> Express your joy in love-making. It boosts your spirits and is an energizing activity. Great sex will leave you feeling good in more ways than one.

Dr. Truth

So many elements of daily life play in to whether or not we are really finding sexual pleasure in our marriage. Sex is not just a technical learning exercise. Sexual techniques are nothing if the heart, mind, and soul are not engaged, if your body isn't healthy, if you aren't respecting your mate, or if you aren't having fun together in many other ways.

Dieting for Sex

Can food help your sex life? Yep. I'm not talking here about the age-old notion of aphrodisiacs, but it's something along those lines. We know now far more about food than we used to. We know a lot more about what our body needs biochemically to function optimally. It shouldn't be any surprise that there are foods you can eat that will help your sex life. Read on!

One thing that inhibits sex is stress. Medical science tells us that when we're stressed our bodies run out of B vitamins. Being anxious, jittery, and stressed depletes our bodily B's. In fact, if you look closely at the vitamin counter you'll find some vitamin products labeled "Stress Formula." These are mixtures of predominantly B vitamins because these are the vitamins that will help you destress. Depressed elderly women are often found to be lacking vitamin B_{12}. In fact, doctors will prescribe B_6 to women for PMS symptoms.

Why? Because the B vitamins will help those nerves to settle down and you will be more relaxed. Eggs are a great source of B vitamins. Other good sources of B vitamins include citrus fruits, greens, chicken, pork, carrots, and fish.

Celery has been said by some to be the "turn-on" vegetable. It's loaded with androstenone and androstenol. These are pheromones (the sexual scent of attraction) that boost your arousal and your spouse's arousal to you. The effect is immediate, so perhaps this is something to add as a "sex snack" in the excitement/romancing phase of your evening together—"Pass the celery, dear." Pheromones are also produced by our own bodies and are responsible for the strange phenomena of women who live together menstruating together. It is our detection of the others pheromones that causes our bodies to recalibrate to each other.

We need energy for sex. Thiamin and riboflavin are good energy vitamins that come fortified in most breakfast cereals. Calcium and phosphorus provide our muscles energy. We need energy for great sex, especially for men whose muscles are involved in controlling ejaculation. Give your muscles a boost before bed—have a glass of milk, chew on a Viactiv caramel, or have some cheese on that celery.

Selenium comes from whole grains, garlic, beef, seafood, eggs, Brazil nuts, and fish. Selenium is found to help prevent prostrate cancer and colorectal problems in men. It has antioxidant qualities and boosts our immune system. It also helps boost the strength of men's sperm (to keep your sperm strong you also want to get adequate amounts of vitamin A, vitamin C, and zinc—are you taking your men's vitamins?). Add some whole-wheat crackers to that "sex snack"!

Keep eating those antioxidants (canned tomatoes, salsa, blueberries, cranberries, garlic, onions, vitamin E, vitamin C, broccoli, sunflower oil, nuts, dairy products, etc.). Antioxidants keep the cholesterol cleaned out of our blood. Cholesterol clogs our blood vessels. If our bodies are going to be able to be orgasmic, blood has to be able to freely flow into our genitals. Men can't have erections without good blood flow. Women's sexual experience will be dampened without good blood flow. Pass the raisins please.

The protein in a good steak will provide a ton of minerals and vitamins that help boost the pleasures of sex.

There is more benefit to eating well than you thought!

Exercising for Sex

The best way to boost your energy reserves is to exercise. Resistance training develops our muscle tissues. Muscle burns calories. The more muscle we develop, the greater our bodies' ability to burn fat and make us feel better.

Are you huffing and puffing during sex? Is your spouse concerned your heart may not be able to take it? Get into some cardiovascular training. You've heard it a hundred times before but here it is again: Walk! Thirty or more minutes a day at least three days a week. Walk at such a pace that you can feel your heart getting a workout but not so hard that you can't continue to talk while walking. The talking is the test. If you're so pooped you can't keep up a conversation with the person walking beside you, you're walking too hard. Slow down!

Regular resistance training will help women prevent osteoporosis in addition to making them more fit for sex.

Everyone who does resistance training and cardio training will (a) feel better, (b) have more energy, and (c) sleep better and require less sleep.

You are going to grow old together. Do you want to be old and sickly? Or old and healthy? It's a choice. The healthier you are the more you will continue to enjoy and develop your sex life.

Chapter 12

Taking Time to Take Care

One of the great things about sex is that it doesn't necessarily end when it's over. The physical connection part may be done, for the time being, but the point of your lovemaking goes beyond the orgasmic moment. Whether your marital sex encounter ends with a bang or something less, there is a spiritual and emotional connection that becomes stronger. That is, if you do the right things after you get out of bed. (After you get out of bed? How about "after the orgasm is over"—you might still be in bed.)

When It Ends with a Bang

Wow! You and your wife just had one hot happy time and now you're both sweaty, heavily breathing, and messes lying in your very unmade bed with huge smiles on your faces. So your next move is to say, "Thanks, honey!" as you jump out of bed and into the shower. Wrong, Bucko! Think again (and the operative word here is *think*).

Unless this was a midday quickie and you both have to get back to work, it's time for the post-game wrap up. There is more to great, loving, marriage-building sex than a big bang. Orgasms are great, but when the good vibrations fade there's still more pleasure to be had.

Think of sex as a great cup of coffee or glass of wine (or whatever your favorite beverage is). You seldom gulp it down in a hurry. It's a special, delicious pleasure to linger over. Part of what makes a great wine great is its sweet bouquet, and the aroma of fresh-brewed coffee is heaven! Sex is better than both and deserves to be savored.

 Word from the Wise

"May God, who gives this patience and encouragement, help you live in complete harmony with each other—each with the attitude of Christ Jesus toward the other." (Romans 15:5) Patience and encouragement are elements of God's character. They are also character elements we need to allow the Holy Spirit to nurture in us. Just as two voices harmonize in a song, they will yield a pleasant harmony in your marriage and sex life.

It's after orgasm that the spiritual connection with your spouse can truly be felt. This is a time of personal, marital, and spiritual thankfulness and a time to experience grace—God's grace and each other's.

As the scripture says, "accept each other as Christ has accepted you; then God will be glorified." It's such a natural thing to praise God and give him thanks after great sex. When it's good, you see what a gift it truly is. We need to be grateful for every good gift from the Lord, and deep intimacy with our spouse is one of those gifts.

There are times when a couple can feel the Lord's presence and blessing during their lovemaking. It can feel like the Father is smiling down on you with great pleasure. There are times when you will offer a silent or spoken prayer during lovemaking—"Thank you, Lord" and "Praise be to God." There is no reason for us to feel we need to hide our nakedness from the Lord, nor hide our lovemaking from him. He is intimately involved with his creation at all times.

Keeping the Glow Going

Sweaty bodies cuddling can be very sexy! The sheets are already mussed and easily washed, so what's the big deal anyway? Linger in your lover's arms and bask in the afterglow. You don't have to speak or do anything else to enjoy the richness of the moment.

It's perfectly natural to want to get into the shower. Women will want to allow the man's ejaculate to drain and both will want to wipe off the sweat. Hold on! There are solutions to these discomforts. For the moment, a few tissues discreetly tucked between the legs will serve well. And putting a towel or two by your bed just before you dive in to sex will take care of the sweat later on. What's the rush? Just being together after orgasm is a wonder in and of itself. Great sex can leave you speechless. It's all the non-verbal, spiritual activity that is still happening after orgasm. Relax. Enjoy. Be.

After a few minutes, you may both need to take quick trips to the bathroom. But make the trip quick and then get back to the cuddling. If you don't really need to, don't rush the ending. This can actually be the best part of making love! It's your time to connect beyond just body to body and appreciate being with each other.

 For Him

Hug her, squeeze her, put your arms around her. Women love to cuddle. Taking the time before and after sex to hold your wife, stroke her arm, snuggle her breasts, will be time well spent. Being physically affectionate with your wife, beyond merely massaging her genitals, will go a long way in building her respect, love, and admiration toward you. It shows her that you love the whole her and aren't just hot for her body.

There really is no "after sex" in marriage. There is only afterglow. Each coupling is one of a series of couplings that will continue until "death do you part." And each coupling builds on all the prior times all working together to more firmly establish the solidity and unity of your marriage. The frequency of sex on this point is irrelevant. More important is the quality of sex when it happens and after it happens.

When It Ends with a Fizzle

All sex is not created equal. There will not always be fireworks nor will the earth move every time. At times, orgasm will be elusive for both the man and the woman. This is normal. There are times when something happens during lovemaking that leaves one or both people feeling awkward, embarrassed, or hurt. There are times that sexual abuse victims will have a flashback when they are making love with their spouse that makes for a really fast fizzle.

The movies, popular songs, TV shows, shower room banter, and many other sources all feed the big lie that all great sex has to be meteorically orgasmic. Every time. It's amazing that, given its unrealistic expectation such a myth persists.

Ignore the myths. Enjoy the truth.

Fatigue and Other Problems

Much of the time, orgasm will happen for both of you one way or another during your lovemaking. But there will be times it won't, even if you're young and healthy. Any number of factors can play into this. Fatigue is a biggie. As much as you like to think of yourselves as Superman and Wonder Woman, you aren't. You're human and you get tired. A really hard, stressful day at the office can sap your energy and lay waste to your libido. So can being home with preschoolers all day.

By itself or added to fatigue, alcohol in any quantity can also have a negative impact, especially on men. Having a cold or the flu, certain medications, an argument the night before, conflict at work, or even being excited and preoccupied with a new challenge can all detract from orgasmic sex. The older you get, the more significant the impact.

It will happen. Right in the middle of lovemaking, the man's penis will go soft or the woman's vagina will dry out. No matter how much will power you exert or stimulation you apply, the results are the same. When it does happen, don't sweat it. Sex without orgasm can still be fulfilling, fun, and connecting. Relax and enjoy each other. Nothing bad has happened. If this is an occasional occurrence, it's normal and okay.

However, if either of you begin having problems becoming or staying aroused on a regular basis, then you probably need to get to a doctor or therapist. Start with the doctor first to rule out any physical problem. (For men who are aren't able to complete orgasm with ejaculation, the experts say that if it goes on for more than three months you need to see a doctor.)

Women can have about 20 different experiences of orgasm. They can have one, two, three, or more orgasms one right after the other. It's amazing what women's bodies can do. But, there will come the day that no matter what you do you can't get an orgasm. In all likelihood you're just plain exhausted. Knowing what your body "can" do can make it frustrating when you can't make it get past the plateau phase to orgasm. In fact, there are times that the plateau phase is so great and lasts so long that it's sex alone that exhausts you to the point you can't get to orgasm. Sometimes it's just going to happen. It's disappointing and frustrating. So close and yet so far! Oh well, what can you do? Keep some humor about yourself—there are things beyond your control.

Various hormonal fluctuations affect men and women. Most of these are transitory and manageable. If the doctor finds nothing, then you need to see a therapist.

A whole range of mental and emotional issues could be behind failing sexual performance. Emotionally, a mild depression brought on by the loss of a loved one or surfacing memories of past abuse could be the culprits. Whether physical or mental, nearly every problem is fixable, and few are unique.

Being Sensitive to Your Spouse

At times like this, the husband should avoid trying to force his wife to continue love-making if she doesn't want to. Let her decide. If she is willing to keep going for your sake, be grateful, courteous, and use some lubricant. Whichever way it goes, take extra time to cuddle, caress, and love your wife. Reassure her that you love her no matter what. Show her that you enjoy just being with her and holding her.

Women need to be sensitive to their husbands as well. Losing an erection can be a big blow to a guy's ego. Manual or oral stimulation may help get things going again. But it may not. If he just can't, let it go. Avoid making a big issue out of it. Cuddle, hug, enjoy the fact that you both have some exclusive time with each other.

The key is to be loving, sensitive, and patient through it all. Even if worst comes to worst and a physical problem makes it impossible for you to have normal intercourse, then you'll just need to get creative!

 For Her

When your husband can't perform, he needs to know that you love him no matter what. He also needs you not to make a big deal out if it. Men's egos are tied up in their ability to perform sexually. He'll be feeling very vulnerable and very frustrated. Warm acceptance and just letting things go will show love to him. In fact, attempting to talk with him about it too soon may not go over well. Hold off. If he can't perform for 2-3 months in a row then express your concern that he may have a medical problem and suggest he see his doctor.

Building Toward the Next Time

Love and sex in marriage is a continuum. In the "Love Chapter," 1 Corinthians 13, Paul wrote, "love is forever." He concludes the chapter with, "There are three things that will endure—faith, hope, and love—and the greatest of these is love." In marriage, love and sex are wrapped up in one bundle. And sex is more than friction between the penis and the vagina.

How you treat your spouse out of bed affects the quality of your relationship in bed. Do you always take time to kiss and hug each other good-bye before heading off to work? Are you polite and courteous at the dinner table? Do you compliment each other from time to time for the little things done around the house or yard? While doing chores around the house, or going to the kitchen for a snack, do you share kisses, hugs, and gentle touches in passing?

Do you share in managing the household, pick up after yourself, help by putting away the dishes, taking out the trash, dusting, sweeping, keeping the living areas of the house straightened up? Do you share the child-rearing responsibilities?

One husband, who left his belongings strewn all over the house, constantly left garbage and molding food in the family car, left his dirty laundry all over the bedroom, left his clean clothes stacked on his dresser, came to bed with a stinky body, and found he had a wife who wasn't too interested in sex. Small wonder! All of these things affect a spouse's desire and interest in sex.

Dr. Truth

Great sex does not happen in a vacuum. Great sex comes out of a marriage that pays attention to the needs of each spouse and the needs of the relationship. Great sex comes from deep love, and daily considerations of your spouse. Anything you do during the day can affect your spouse and their desire for intimacy with you. Remember, sex starts in the mind.

Do you spend a few minutes each day chatting with each other and keeping up with what's happening in your lives? Are there a couple of TV shows you enjoy watching together? A favorite author you both read or a music group you both like to listen to? Perhaps you both like to listen to "A Prairie Home Companion" on Saturday nights or rent an action movie for the weekend. Is there at least one thing that you don't particularly enjoy doing, but that you do with your spouse anyway because it's something they enjoy?

All these behaviors and more help you build a positive basis for great lovemaking.

Great lovemaking comes out of a great marriage. While there are couples who have disastrous marriages yet have great sex, this is by far the exception rather than the rule. Most often disastrous marriages have disastrous sex lives, if they have any sex life at all. A marriage is created by the union of two whole people. When one or both of you come into marriage fractured from the past you will need to do your own healing work before the marriage will become whole.

Sad was the day I saw a couple who was having trouble in their sex lives. The husband was complaining that his wife never wanted to have sex. It didn't take long to discover that this man was so full of anger that he could hardly contain himself. He said he was angry because she wouldn't have sex. She said she wouldn't have sex because of his anger. This was a man whose issues went far beyond his wife's rebuffs. He had issues he had to deal with long before he and his wife could address the lack of sex in their marriage.

Even those who are fairly healthy emotionally when they enter marriage find that marriage is a lot of work. Good relationships develop and grow over time when two people are both committed to dealing with all of the problematic issues. Slowly but surely, when we pursue healing for ourselves and our marriage, we develop a great marriage. Great lovemaking will develop as the marriage develops.

In addition to taking care of each other's needs, you also need to take care of yourself. Eating healthy and getting at least a little bit of exercise is important. Exercising your spiritual muscles with regular personal Bible reading and devotional time also is crucial to great sex.

There's a lot that you can easily neglect to take care of that, without realizing it, has a direct effect on how hot of a time you have in bed with your spouse.

Word from the Wise

"What a lovely, pleasant sight you are, my love, as we lie here on the grass, shaded by cedar trees and spreading firs." (Song of Songs 1:16)

When the fireworks fade and the breathing slows down, take time to just be with your spouse and enjoy who they are. Let your heart fill with gratitude that God has given you to each other.

Part 3

All About Kids

Sex leads to pregnancy, which leads to birth, which leads to kids. Having children is a wonderful experience. But kids, whatever their age, will have an impact on your sex life. As babies, they'll keep you awake through the night as you lovingly care for their needs. When they get older, privacy becomes more of an issue.

In blended families, there are special challenges that the husband and wife need to deal with. There will also be adjustments when the kids leave, when they come back for a visit, or if they move back in.

Keeping the Kids Out of the Bedroom

When kids are present in a marriage, things become very different. Whether they're newborns, toddlers, teens, or even young adults, children present new challenges that can impinge on the sexual intimacy of the husband and wife.

Starting Again After Giving Birth

There are three primary issues that arise for a woman's health after pregnancy: (1) resumption of sexual activity, (2) Postpartum depression, (3) physical vulnerability to long-term damage to joints, muscles, and tendons.

Resuming Sexual Activity

You should avoid vaginal intercourse after childbirth until all bleeding has stopped. This generally takes four to six weeks if the new mother has been taking care of herself and not overdoing it.

Some young mothers are just too anxious to get back to "normal" after the delivery and when they notice their bleeding tapering off substantially, they overexert themselves in some way. They wake up the next morning to find out that the bleeding has significantly increased. The healing process has now been delayed by a week or two. You are not doing yourself, your baby, or your husband a favor by doing things your body can't handle yet.

Your uterus needs time to get back to normal. Stop and think: Normally, the uterus is the size of a clenched fist. During pregnancy your uterus grew big enough to hold your baby, the placenta, and tons of fluid. It takes time (six weeks) for it to recover. You can help your uterus to shrink by doing two things: breast-feed your baby and massage your tummy regularly. Breast-feeding stimulates your hormones; you will feel your uterus contracting as you nurse. You will be nursing according to when your baby is hungry. In between feedings, if you put your hand on your tummy and begin to massage it, you will also feel your uterus become tight and hard inside your tummy. You will feel the after pains (the pain that comes as the uterus contracts). The more the uterus contracts, the faster it gets back to normal size and the faster you stop bleeding. Short-term pain for quicker healing.

All of the bleeding and discharge you experience isn't from the uterus. The vagina has just had a baby work its way through the birth canal. Sometimes the inner mucous walls of the vagina sustain tears and bruising. The vagina could take up to eight weeks to completely heal.

Sometimes little clots of blood are still coming out from the uterus. This is also normal. For all this blood and discharge, use a pad, not a tampon. You do not want to block or trap all this discharge in the vagina. You do not want to irritate your vagina; it is trying to heal. You will risk infections (hence more vaginal trouble) if you use tampons after childbirth.

Did you have an episiotomy? You want to let that heal, too. The episiotomy cut is made in the perineum. The perineum is part of muscle system that works its way in a figure 8 around your urethra, your vagina and your anus. You want it to heal properly. Having sex prematurely could rupture your episiotomy and that would be terribly painful and could require more stitches.

Ask yourself this question: How soon do we want another baby? Friends of mine went for their six-week check up (the check-up you're supposed to get for the okay from the doctor to resume sex) and the doctor told them they were pregnant again! The babies were born 10 months apart. Just because you've just had a baby doesn't mean you aren't fertile yet to have another one. Wait for the doctor's okay and then think about how soon you want another baby and use birth control to help your plan be a success.

You've got the picture—don't have sex until everything down there is healed and the doctor gives you the okay. Or, positively stated, when everything is healed, you can start enjoying sex again.

Hey, this doesn't mean you should stop the hugging, kissing, cuddling, and nuzzling. Lots of loving is possible without vaginal intercourse.

Postpartum Depression

After childbirth your body is trying to get back to normal in every way. Your hormones play a huge role in this. While you may have especially enjoyed pregnancy in terms of more steady emotions, post-pregnancy will be the wildest time for your body hormonally.

There are some women who report virtually no concerns about depression at all after their babies are born. There are other women who experience such deep postpartum depression that they become a threat to themselves and their children.

Both mother and father must take responsibility for noticing postpartum depression symptoms and getting necessary medical and psychological help immediately. Diagnostic criteria for depression include: (1) feelings of depression every day or nearly every day or (2) loss of interest in every or nearly every usual life activity for at least two weeks. In addition, there must be at least four of the following symptoms: significant weight loss or weight gain; inability to sleep or sleeping all the time; fidgety agitation or really slowed movements nearly every day; fatigue or loss of energy nearly every day; feeling worthless or inappropriately guilty nearly every day; decreased ability to think, concentrate, or make decisions nearly every day; recurrent thoughts of death or wishing one was dead.

If the new mother has these symptoms, get her directly to her doctor for both medication and a referral to a mental health professional.

Care for Your Muscles

Another often-unmentioned concern for women after delivery is the care of their muscles, ligaments, and tendons.

Try to help your wife for two to three months after your baby has been born. Before your baby was born, your wife's muscles began loosening and relaxing to make it possible for her pelvic bones to shift to allow your child to come through the birth canal. The thing is, it's not just the muscles in the pelvic area that loosen and soften up—it happens to the entire body. It takes a full three months for all of these muscles to firm up again after delivery.

Even though your wife has energy and drive to do things, she could still sustain life-long injuries if she strains any muscles during this time. If she is injured, her body won't be able to put itself back together quite the way it was originally. Women in midlife can point to the pain they feel from the injuries sustained in the first few months after their baby was born. Women need to take care with themselves during this time, and their husbands need to also pay attention to this and pitch in.

Word from the Wise

"You will be able to tell wonderful stories to your children and grandchildren about the marvelous things I am doing among the Egyptians to prove that I am the LORD." (Exodus 10:2)

One of the greatest joys of having children is passing onto them your Christian heritage, to instill in them the truths and values of the Bible. God not only worked among the Egyptians but works in you and your children's lives today. One way to do this is to share with them your own stories of faith over the years.

Finding Time When They're Young

Becoming a parent will truly change your life. There is nothing like it. When you hold your son or daughter in your hands for the first time, you will be love struck! A tiny baby can cause the biggest man to tear up and coo. For the first few moments and days, all the doubts, fears, and intimidation that came with the thought of becoming a first-time mom and dad fade completely away. Your newborn child is nothing but a bundle of joy, fascination, and pride.

But that all changes after a few turns at changing diapers at responding to cries of hunger at 3 o'clock in the morning. Morning after morning after morning after … well, you get the idea.

If you thought it felt a little crowded as a newlywed, as you adjusted to living with another adult who seemed to be around all the time, wait'll you get the new baby home! It will seem as if your entire life is now totally consumed by care for your new baby.

However, while it is appropriate and necessary to spend a lot of time and energy caring for your child, it should not take up every minute of every day and night. It's important to make sure there is still dedicated time for mom and dad to be affectionate with each other.

In the first few weeks when intercourse is not possible, you can still enjoy cuddling and fondling. Even if the baby starts crying, you do not need to jump up immediately. Wait and listen. The cries might fade if the baby goes back to sleep.

Scheduling Alone Time

To avoid parental burnout you will need to make time for yourselves. As much as you may not want to part from your little bundle, your child will not be scarred for life if you hire a babysitter or leave him or her with grandma. Schedule a few hours on the weekend or an evening during the week for a date. Book your babysitter (or grandparents) in advance so they will know that you expect them to help you each week.

If you hire a babysitter, you'll want to have them come to your house to watch the baby while you go to dinner and a movie, or shopping, or book a hotel room for a few hours. If grandparents who are nearby are the sitters, you may want to take the baby to them so you can have your house, and bedroom, all to yourself.

The key is to schedule time alone and then take it. Maintaining your intimacy and closeness keeps your marriage strong and allows you to be better parents. Failing to care for your marriage will create tension and stress that your baby or toddler will pick up on.

 For Him

Despite how it's presented in sitcoms, changing a diaper is not a big deal. With the convenience of disposable diapers and sanitary wipes, it's a snap to make your baby boy or girl comfortable with a clean, fresh, dry diaper. Think of it as a priceless opportunity to bond with and demonstrate your love for your baby. Don't make your wife do all of the "dirty" work! If you're a little unsure of how to manage, watch your wife and ask questions.

Separate Room, Separate Bed

Unless there is some urgent medical reason that requires constant care and vigilance, it is generally not necessary to keep the baby in the same room with you. Get a baby monitor and turn it to a volume such that you can hear crying but not every whimper. You still both need your privacy and you need to be able to sleep at night. You can agree to take turns getting up at night for feedings so that one of you can continue to get rest. If your wife is breast-feeding, after she nurses the baby, let her get back to sleep while you change your baby's diaper. Your baby shouldn't be in the room when you are being intimate. It can be more than just a little distracting and your focus at these times needs to be on each other.

It can also be distracting for the child if he or she is tired and trying to sleep. The noises and movement mommy and daddy are making will not be conducive to a peaceful sleep for the tot. They need a little privacy, too!

It is also not a good idea to allow your baby (or toddler) to sleep in the same bed as you and your husband. Experts agree that this is actually very dangerous for the child. You and your husband probably move around much more than you realize in your sleep. Too many parents who had their baby in bed with them have awakened to the horror of finding their precious child dead—because one of them rolled over on the baby without being aware of it. How tragic.

Also, once you allow a child to feel as if your bedroom is also his or her bedroom, as they get older it will be even more difficult to maintain your privacy. One of the fun things about married sex is the fact that it can happen any time! You and your spouse could both wake up in the middle of the night and decide to make love. It's a great way to help you get back to sleep afterwards! Always having a child in your bed will put the kibosh on any such activity.

From time to time as the child grows, he or she may want to sleep with mommy and daddy because he or she is afraid or not feeling well, or just a little lonely. It's okay to let the child spend a few minutes in bed as you comfort and reassure him or her. As he or she settles down, take him or her back to his or her room and his or her bed, place him or her in it, and spend a few more minutes reassuring and even praying with him or her. Establishing this practice as your normal routine early on will actually serve as a point of comfort to the child. Children prefer consistency. They are most comfortable when they know what to expect. This procedure tells them it's okay to come into mom and dad's bedroom when they need comforting, but that they will always sleep in their own room and bed.

As a marriage therapist, I'm aware that when couples tell me that one of their children is sleeping in their bed, it is usually a tactic consciously or subconsciously used by one spouse to keep sexually separate from the other. In other words, it's a clear sign of marriage problems. If your spouse starts wanting your child to sleep in your marriage bed it's time to start talking or to consult with a counselor or your pastor. Children should not be used in any way to keep a couple from dealing with their issues.

As They Get Older (and More Curious)

It's truly exciting to watch your child take his or her first step or hear him or her speak his or her first word. But the novelty of those moments will wear off. Soon they are into everything and jabbering nonstop a mile a minute. Plus, since everything around is brand new, their curiosity is operating at full throttle. They will ask you about anything and everything, and they will say whatever pops into their head.

Keep in mind a few truths about children: Even when they appear to be preoccupied with a toy or activity, they hear everything you say. As they learn to talk, they mimic what they hear. Kids vary in how articulate they are, or rather, how good they are at mimicking what they hear adults say.

Some parents can become fairly intimidated by an articulate child. It's easy to get caught up in a "conversation" with the child and forget that he or she is just a child. Forgetting this can lead a parent to have unrealistic expectations of the child. For instance, a parent may believe their child can reason and understand better than they actually can. This can result in frustration for both parent and child.

When a child starts asking questions about sexuality, be sure you understand exactly what he or she is asking. It may sound as if they are aware of more than they are, or that they want expansive, detailed information. In reality, they probably have something very simple in mind. For instance, if a girl has seen a naked boy baby, she may recognize that the boy has a penis and she does not. A simple answer, such as God made boys and girls different, may be all that is required. Launching into a detailed explanation and anatomy is not required for a toddler, and could overwhelm and even confuse the child.

At each stage of development children need to be given age-appropriate information about their bodies and the bodies of the opposite sex. Children need to learn while young that their bodies are for their own enjoyment and for them to share with their spouse when they get married and with nobody else. As we teach children about their bodies we also need to be teaching them about protecting their bodies from inappropriate or unwanted touch by others. The older they get the more details of the physiology of their bodies needs to be taught and a full knowledge of conception needs to be explained. We also need to be talking with our kids, long before the teen years, about what appropriate boundaries there should be in dating and how to handle it if their date tries to push them beyond their convictions and conscience. Consult a couple of good books by reputable authors, or even talk to a therapist if you are unsure how much to tell your child about sex. Consult your Christian bookstore for solid books on a Christian approach to telling your kids about sex.

The old assumption among many Christians has been the less a child or teen knows about sex, the better. This is completely untrue. A lack of knowledge actually produces more curiosity and exploration (and possibly rebellion). Your children will get the information somewhere. Better that it comes from you, presented lovingly and in the context of our Christian faith, than that they learn it from non-Christian friends.

Knowing about sex coupled with Christian values and biblical truths will equip your child to better deflect an inappropriate sexual advance. The knowledge can help provide a safeguard from molestation as a child or being seduced as a teen.

Knowing the truth about their bodies and sex, and understanding that the changes they will go through are perfectly normal, will alleviate a lot of their fear and awkwardness. It will lessen the chance for them to develop unhealthy issues or shame regarding sex. It will also help in key areas like pornography and masturbation.

For Her

Open the communication between yourself and your children about sexual issues from a young age. Don't wait for your kids to come to you to ask questions. At each stage of their lives you need to be providing information and guidance. If you let your kids know that these conversations are a-okay with you, when they have a question, a concern, or a problem about something pertaining to sex, they'll feel they can come to you. Kids listen even when they appear to be ignoring you.

When It's None of Their Business

Still, despite their growing curiosity, what goes on between you and your spouse sexually is none of their business. They do not need to be given any details of your sex life. As boys and girls get older, they will need increasing privacy and parents need to keep themselves covered. Dad, no more walking around the house in your underwear. Mom, put a robe over that negligee. And when you are in the bedroom together or in a shared bathroom, keep the door locked. Always!

Having a child walk in on you when you are nude or in the act is embarrassing for you and can be traumatic for them. If it happens though, don't overreact. Explain that they need to knock and wait to be invited in before entering your bedroom. If they surprise you in the bathroom, apologize to them for not locking the door.

Ultimately, set clear boundaries for your children when it comes to your privacy. A parent will always have the right (and responsibility) to go into a child's room when they are not around for any number of reasons. It's also okay to enter a young child's room when they are in the room, but as they get older the parent needs to knock first. It is not appropriate to insist that an older child or teen always leave their bedroom door open when dressing or sleeping. If there is some legitimate reason for entering an older child's or a teen's room when they are in the room, it is generally best if the same-sex parent does it. A parent should never sleep in the child's room with their child, no matter how mad they might be at their spouse!

The child needs to know to stay out of the parents' room all the time unless given express permission. Your bedroom is your private sanctuary and boudoir! Let your children know that they may come in if they are invited, and only if they are invited.

Dr. Truth

> Young children often wake up much earlier than their parents. Once awake, they want to know what mommy and daddy are doing and may come looking for you. Even with your door locked, they may be insistent about getting in. A solution is to put a clock in their room. Draw a picture of the clock with the hands (or digital numbers) indicating the time you will be up. Tell your child that until the clock matches the sign, they are to stay in their room and play. Or get a clock radio and set the radio to come on. Either way, they'll usually be fine knowing that they can knock on your bedroom door at the right time and you will welcome them in. Before that, you and your spouse can enjoy each other in privacy.

Other areas of your lives, in addition to your sex lives, should also remain off limits to your kids. They do not need to know every detail of what is going on between you and your spouse. Teach your children to respect your privacy just as they want you to respect theirs. Do not confide in your children as if they were an adult friend. Never lose sight of your roles: You are the parents and they are the children.

Never share with a child something your spouse has specifically asked you not to. Respect each other's wishes in this area. Even if you see no harm in sharing, your spouse does, and the child probably doesn't really need to know. Work out with your spouse what you both agree is reasonable to share with the kids. If you're not sure on a specific item, wait and talk to your spouse first before blabbing. Err on the side of caution.

Kids have enough to deal with as they grow up. They don't need to be burdened with your adult issues, problems, and fears. Part of parenting is knowing when to protect children from learning too much too soon, while at the same time ensuring they do know what they need to know. It's a balancing act, to be sure, but with the discernment of the Holy Spirit and having the mind of Christ, you'll do fine.

Word from the Wise

"Teach your children to choose the right path, and when they are older, they will remain upon it." (Proverbs 22:6)

What a joy it is to see your children enter their adult years as virgins, committed to abstinence before marriage and watching out to avoid situations that could compromise their sexuality. Job well done!

Chapter 14

His Kids, Her Kids

Sex and the blended family brings a few added challenges that can affect the quality of your sex life. If not handled properly, your times in bed will be more debate and argument than fun and fooling around. The good news is that the issues are not insurmountable.

It's the Same, but Different

A blended family is when persons from one family come together with persons of another family through marriage. This happens when a man or woman, with or without children, divorced or widowed, marries another person who may or may not have been previously married, and who may or may not have children of their own.

In some ways blended families are no different from nuclear families. There are still two parents although one or both may be a stepparent. Anyone observing the blended family on an outing would not know the difference by just looking at them.

For those in the blended family, however, the new situation feels much more different than what they experienced previously. A stepparent can feel like and be viewed as an outsider. If children are involved on both sides, everyone can feel as if their space is being invaded.

Differences in all areas surface quickly. One family may have been used to always saying please and thank you at the dinner table, while the other merely stated pass this or that. What is considered humorous by one side is considered insensitive by the other. His family folded towels lengthwise while her family folded them across their width. Her family opened Christmas gifts on Christmas morning between 8 A.M. and 11 A.M. His family always opened at least one gift each on Christmas Eve and as soon as the kids got up on Christmas morning. From the profound to the mundane, culture clash will be everywhere. Everyone will be adjusting to the new situation.

For the newlyweds, this is a double whammy. In their prior marriages there were no kids around in the beginning. They had all the privacy they could want. No one was there to hear and comment on arguments. They didn't have to be quiet while making love or get dressed to go to the fridge in the middle of the night. Getting to know each other and working through all the issues that come with a new marriage was done just between the spouses. Now, everyone's in on the action and everyone has an opinion about every overheard word.

The kids have it hard, too. While a little storming is normal for a couple at the start of a marriage, for kids it can seem like World War III every time a voice is raised. If a discussion gets heated with the kids around, they are very likely to jump in and defend their biological parent against the "intruder." They may feel like their new world is falling apart right away just like their old one did.

Word from the Wise

"Jacob was the father of Joseph, the husband of Mary. Mary was the mother of Jesus, who is called the Messiah." (Matthew 1:16)

"Then he returned to Nazareth with them and was obedient to them; and his mother stored all these things in her heart." (Luke 2:51)

It's sometimes difficult for older stepchildren to respect and accept the authority of their stepparent. Joseph was not the father of Jesus. He was very much like a stepfather. Even knowing this, as he surely did, Jesus did not view Joseph except as a father. He was respectful and obedient to both Mary and Joseph. It may be helpful for the biological parent to explain this to his or her children, and, lovingly, make it clear that the stepparent is to be respected and obeyed. It's equally important for the stepparent to at all times be sensitive, loving, and patient with the new kids in the house.

The kids know that the stepparent isn't their "real" father or mother. In Jesus' situation, he was with Joseph from the beginning. Joseph was the only human father he knew.

Jesus wasn't getting used to a new father part way through his life. The younger children are when a remarriage occurs, the more opportunity they have to grow into a relationship with their stepparent. When remarriage comes when the kids are teens, they have a short time to be at home with their stepparent before they leave home. There is not the same amount of time to invest in the stepparent/stepchild relationship.

The blended family is quite a challenge. The spouse who has kids living with them needs to parent their children and develop a new marriage with their new spouse. Children can get resentful of the time you are putting into the new spouse and the new spouse can get resentful of the time you put into your kids. It's a juggling act. Everybody wants a piece of you now. Your spouse didn't get married to be alone. Your kids don't want to share you. You need to continue parenting while developing your new marriage.

Part of developing the new marriage is working on your sex life. As mentioned, this can be a challenge. It can be quite a shock to find out that people sitting in the room downstairs can hear when your bed creeks and they know you're making out. Keep the bed oiled! It can be disturbing for kids to go by the bedroom door and hear groaning. Insulate! You might find that you have to make love after the kids go to school or when they are out with their friends, or in bed sound asleep.

It's hard for children to think of their parent with another spouse. Even if they understand why the previous marriage ended and would never want that marriage rejoined, it's still hard for kids to have a stepparent. The whole idea of intimacy between a kid's parents is something kids don't want to think about. This feeling is even more intense when a stepparent is involved. Discretion is even more necessary in a stepfamily than it was in the original family.

Years after Sybil's father died she asked her mom if she and her dad ever had sex. She was surprised when her mom replied, "Do you ever stop?" They had been married 28 years. That's how discreet they were. Sex between a married couple is not something we put before children. Period. Sex is for the adults, in private. It doesn't involve the kids.

The remarried couple with children may need to make extra effort to develop their sex lives. You may have to put more planning into when the kids go to see their other parent. If there are his kids and her kids, see if you can arrange some of the visits to all occur at the same time now and then. Farm the kids out all at friends' houses once a month on the same day. Or have someone come in for a night and you go out to a nice hotel.

Who's in Charge When

Being a stepparent is hard. Especially if all the kids in the house are stepkids. You are a parent, yet not a parent. They are "your" kids but not your kids. If the child is very young, the transition will be easier and their affection will grow more evenly toward both parent and stepparent. Older kids, especially teens, are different. They may tend to gravitate toward the biological parent whenever they have a question. Depending on their ages, they may tend to rebuff any affection you show them.

Discipline will also be an issue. As a stepparent, your authority may be challenged aggressively. Your experience of the kids can be radically different than the experience of the biological parent.

Working through these and other issues requires a lot of communication, patience, and understanding between you and your spouse. As the biological parent, be sensitive when your spouse raises a concern and try really hard to see things from their perspective. As the stepparent, tread lightly in the first several months until the kids become more used to you and have a better grasp of who you are as a person.

Experts say there is about a two-year transition period for the blended family. At the beginning of the marriage the parent should do all the disciplining and the stepparent should focus solidly on relationship building with the stepkids. As the first year of marriage draws to an end, the stepparent can begin to discipline in small things and over the next year become more and more involved with the parent in the equitable disciplining of the children.

One family in counseling was having trouble between the mother's teenage daughter and her stepdad, who was very strict. Contributing to the girl's rebellion against him was the fact that she had been only eight years old when he married her mother and had immediately assumed the role of disciplinarian. In the child's eyes he wasn't her father and had no right to discipline her. He had not invested time in building a positive relationship with her. Because the mother permitted his actions, the daughter lost respect for her, too. Counseling involved making opportunities for the stepdad to have positive encounters with the daughter, and mom had to be the one who announced the ground rules for her behavior. Slowly, things began to turn around. Stepparents can't step into the role of disciplinarian before the family is ready for it.

Be in agreement on issues of discipline, and be consistent. Once you've agreed to a course of action, stick to it and fully support each other.

A standard practice with kids is to play one parent against the other. It happens in all families. We've all done it. Be especially alert to this happening in a blended family. When approached by a kid claiming that the other parent agreed to such and such, check with your spouse before you render a decision. In fact, you will need to check with each other and discuss issues far more frequently than occurs in a nuclear family.

Why? Again, in a nuclear family the husband and wife start off with no children around. They usually have time to get to know each other well before kids come along, or at least before the kids are old enough to be really aware of what's going on. Over time, as you all grow together, you develop your own unique husband-to-wife and parent-to-child communication. You have shared experiences spanning years. The "new-comer" does not have the benefit of this shared experience, and the husband and wife are in the process of learning their own new unique language.

 For Him and Her

> If you've both brought children into the marriage, you will need to work overtime to ensure that none are treated more favorably than others by either of you. Showing "blood" favoritism will only drive a wedge between all members of both sides. Your spouse and step-kids will begin to resent you and your kids. Listen to your spouse when they point out issues and work together to make all of your children feel loved and included in your new family.

It's a good idea to consult a family therapist if things get tough. An outside objective party might need to be involved for a number of reasons: the intensity of attachment to our own children and how much we want to defend our own children; we have never learned to share parenting since we have always done it by ourselves; we might have baggage about our old spouse that we are putting on our new spouse; if our kids were abused by our former spouse we may have excessive fears of our new spouse potentially abusing our kids and may not be able to give our new spouse a fair chance.

Making use of a family therapist can also give the kids a place to be heard and give them an outside, objective party who can reiterate some of the things that their parents may be telling them but which they don't want to hear from their parents. The family therapist can help the kids to deal with their inner turmoil about their parent getting remarried and any issues they have with their stepparents.

Remember, none of us has all the answers. Sometimes in life we find ourselves in situations we aren't prepared for. It is a strong person who knows when they are out of their league and engages an expert to help (whether it's over taxes, gardening, or kids).

Bringing up issues about the kids will quash intimacy, immediately. Blended families have way more "kid" issues (um, make that "parenting" issues). Because the tendency will be to find fault with your spouse's kids and defend your own kids, it's not wise to enter such a minefield before bed. It's a surefire way to create a rotten night. This won't just create tension before you go to sleep, it may keep you from falling asleep and having a good sleep. Parenting issues are better dealt with when there is sufficient time to deal with the issues and at a time that won't disrupt your sleeping. It goes without saying that if you have planned a time of intimacy with your new spouse, don't even utter a word about the kids once your time for intimacy has begun.

When the Kids Are Grossed Out by the Newcomer

Most kids, while intellectually able to acknowledge that moms and dads, well, you know, do it, they generally aren't comfortable really knowing that it occurs. Even kissing in front of the kids can gross them out.

When a new stepparent comes on the scene, the idea of their parent having sex with the newcomer not only grosses them out, but can also be just too painful to acknowledge.

Here you are, a newlywed, who may want to have tons and tons of sex with your new spouse and you have to exercise restraint and work around the entire family (kids, work, spouse).

Sex between spouses in a blended family, out of necessity, will need to be far more discreet. Every noise that comes out of your bedroom, even if it's just a loud yawn, may be interpreted as sexual activity if overheard by the kids, and create emotional tension. Be considerate, and when making love, be quiet. If your bedroom is upstairs over the family room, make sure the kids are watching TV before you start making the bed springs and floorboards squeak!

There may also be negative reactions to any public display of affection between you and your spouse. Here's where you need to draw the line and put the kids on the other side of it. As long as you and your spouse are not passionately making out, the kids need to keep their thoughts to themselves. There is nothing wrong with holding hands, sitting next to each other on the couch, hugging in the kitchen, or lightly kissing your spouse in front of the kids. If the kids get upset and make rude remarks expressing their displeasure, let them know that if they are uncomfortable they can leave the room. However, you should also not be doing this behavior just to annoy or aggravate them. They will sense the difference. If they sense you are just trying to aggravate them it will engender anger in them. Please consider your children and their feelings. If they sense your actions are out of love for their parent they will adjust but it'll take a few years.

Eventually they'll get used to the little affections you show one another, and even begin to appreciate your behavior knowing that it's a visible indication that the marriage is stable and healthy. It's the same in families where kids have both their parents still married. They may say that they are uncomfortable when their parents hug or kiss each other in front of them but inside, it also gives them a feeling of security about the marriage and the stability of their family.

For Her

Feeling that pull between your new husband and your children (and his) can cause women a lot of stress. Often mothers are the central communication switchboard in a family. You may be asked to communicate information from your husband to your kids and his and back. Mothers may be trying to keep the peace with everyone while breaking up inside. If this leaves you feeling frazzled it's time to direct "the children" and "the husband" to speak to each other directly and deal with each other.

Be encouraged—in the same way that couples without children take a couple of years to really adjust with each other, your new marriage will take about the same amount of time or perhaps even a year longer. The road does get smoother. The kids do grow up and you will find time to enjoy the new man in your life.

Remember, you have married each other now because you fell in love and you sensed before God that his blessing was with your union. Even though your kids might not totally understand why you got married again, they need to know that you have a right to adult companionship and love. The kids may have felt you were alright together, just you and them. Remind them that the Lord said it was not good for man to be alone. The Lord created men and women to find wholeness in one another in marriage. Remind them that one day they will grow up and leave home. When that happens you want someone in your life to love and be loved by, that you want to share your life with another and that you want to grow old together with someone you've spent many years of your life with.

Keeping Them in Their Places, with Love

It can be confusing for kids to live with a new stepparent and learn new ways of doing things. What was allowed before may not be now, or vice versa. If one spouse was a single parent for a number of years, or their former spouse was uninvolved in the parenting of their children, discipline may have been lax. This can happen because the single-parent is stretched thin with earning a living and taking care of kids and a household. Kids will naturally push the envelope toward getting their own way, and a tired, overworked parent can be easy prey.

Now, supported by a new spouse who shares their values and the workload, it may become apparent that some of the rules for the kids need to be adjusted. Children of all ages need boundaries and limits and don't do well imposing these on themselves. That's what parents are for. While the kids may lament that any shift in the rules is "Unfair!" the issue isn't about fairness but their well-being. If both parent and stepparent are in agreement and stand firm, and the shift is not harsh, the kids will adjust and eventually appreciate the new way of doing things. (Think small changes over a longer period of time. Drastic changes in rules or guidelines will put your kids in a tailspin and engender unnecessary rebelliousness.) Over time as they see consistency and love behind the rules, they'll grow into the rules, then they'll chill out.

Dr. Truth

Stepfathers need to be sensitive to privacy issues related to stepdaughters. Likewise stepmoms need to be careful in their relationship with stepsons. This is especially true when the kids are teens. The boundaries and roles need to be kept clear at all times.

Lines need to be clear between the kids, too. A teen boy can develop a crush on his teen stepsister, and vice versa. The parents need to be alert and help keep the relationships clear. If any inappropriate behavior is detected, it needs to be dealt with promptly and lovingly. Dads should talk to the boys and moms should talk to the girls about these issues.

When you start coming together with your spouse on issues related to the kids you'll notice that your times of intimacy are no longer getting sabotaged over conversations and conflicts over the kids. As parents in a blended family you must find a way to come together over issues pertaining to the kids and you must do it fairly quickly without trying to be dominating or controlling over the other spouse. If there are too many fights over kids, it's time to book an appointment with a family therapist for help. Conflict over kids can be the end of a potentially good marriage or can seriously damage your relationship with the kids. Don't let this happen to your new family.

 Word from the Wise

"But those who live to please the Spirit will harvest everlasting life from the Spirit. So don't get tired of doing what is good. Don't get discouraged and give up, for we will reap a harvest of blessing at the appropriate time." (Galatians 6:8-9)

It is the Spirit of God whom we should please. The work it takes to blend a family cannot be underestimated. It is a big project and can be taxing. But, if we are seeking the Lord, if we are living in submission to him, if we know we have followed his voice in remarriage, then we must continue to hold to the things he's shown us and not get discouraged or give up. We must do all of the human things necessary to bring our family into harmony and peace before God. We will reap his blessing.

Chapter 15

After Kids: The Good, the Bad, the Ugly

You love your kids to death but there comes a time when they need to go. But then sometimes they come back. Of course, when they're only going for a visit to your former spouse's house or the grandparents' place, it's a good thing when they come back. Otherwise, the goings and comings can be a mixed bag.

Sharing the Kids

Having to "share" your children with a parent from whom you are divorced can be tough. Regardless of the reasons behind the divorce, it will surely be a tad uncomfortable having to remain in contact with your former spouse. It may also be annoying to hear your kids talk about their other parent, especially if they have had a really great time with them.

It can create a little discomfort for your new spouse, as well. Given the somewhat tenuous position he or she holds with your kids, it can be awkward having to deal with the fact that the kids have a "real" mom or dad.

The kids, too, will have plenty of issues to deal with. They love their noncustodial parent, but they can feel stifled in expressing that in front of the stepparent. And even if they have a great time when visiting the noncustodial parent, the bulk of their life is happening in your house.

All of these and more are issues that you and your new spouse need to talk about and be sensitive to. From time to time, one or both of you, and each of the kids, may need to sit down with a therapist to work through some of the tougher ones. Your pastor can also provide strong biblical counseling in this area.

But while there are challenges, there are also positives. If the situation means that all of the children in the house are gone at the same time, it's your chance to continue the honeymoon!

Plan ahead. Go somewhere for the weekend (be sure you give your former spouse the contact information and let your kids know you will still be reachable) or just go overnight to a nearby hotel. Make sure work projects won't keep you late during the week or require you to go in on weekends. If you can't manage it any other time, make sure that when the kids are gone for a visitation that you and your spouse are locked into one or more dates.

With the house to yourselves, you can make love wherever you want as loud as you want as often as you are able. Don't miss the opportunity!

Word from the Wise

"This explains why a man leaves his father and mother and is joined to his wife, and the two are united into one." (Genesis 2:24)

From the very beginning God ordained marriage. Becoming a couple requires leaving parents and becoming one with your new spouse, starting your own home with your own new family.

When the Kids Are Grown and Gone

If you aren't in a blended marriage and children are around or will be, then your times alone may be fewer and far between. Of course, there are the occasional weekend sleepovers at a friend's house and camp in the summers.

However, for nearly all parents, there comes that day when the kids are all grown, through college, and living on their own in their own houses or apartments.

Can you spell p-a-r-t-y? It's mom and dad's turn to shake it up without interference from the small fry. But before you decide to institute streaking through the house followed by sex on the couch as a regular routine, you may need to prepare first.

Even though your children are now adults, on their own, and out of your house, you may still want to have some rules in place. A big one might be to insist that they call before dropping by. For some families this courtesy is a given. For others, the accepted practice may be to just show up on each other's doorstep without warning. While that seems neighborly and all, it does have its risks. Especially if you want to do the streaking thing!

Make sure whatever your accepted custom is that you explain a few things to your children. If just showing up is okay, then at least insist that they don't just let themselves in. They need to knock first and give you time to come to the door.

When the grandkids come along, if you live nearby you will undoubtedly be recruited for babysitting duty—and you'll love it! You and your husband also still need to protect your private time to maintain your intimacy. Before it becomes an issue, be proactive and sit down with your married and pregnant kids and work out some guidelines regarding babysitting. Perhaps you will want to reserve one block of time each week when you are not available unless it's a dire emergency. This will remind your kids that they need to have back-up babysitters available and that dumping of kids without warning is a no-no.

Another thing to consider is what your expectations are. Are they realistic or are you thinking sex without the kids around is going to be just like it was 25 years ago? Think about it. Certain aspects of your sexual experience will improve with time and experience. Others will not. Frequency and duration, especially for men, most likely will be affected. Also, as men get older, becoming aroused takes longer and erections may not be as solid as before.

Still, great sex awaits empty-nesters! So what if things take a little longer to happen? You can fool around all evening and no one is going to interrupt you!

Imagine lying on the couch together, naked under a blanket, watching your favorite shows while twiddling gently with each other. Who knew commercials were made for orgasms!

 For Him

When the kids are gone and retirement is looming, don't forget your wife. The new found freedom you are about to experience isn't all just for you. As you daydream about new hobbies or travel, think of ways to include your wife. Talk to her and learn what her dreams for your sunset years may be. Work together to ensure you both will be satisfied with your choices.

When the Kids Come Back

It happens a lot anymore. Adult children go out into the world and encounter a debilitating bump that sends them reeling all the way back home. In most instances what happens is beyond their control, such as the sudden downsizing of their workplace, a serious illness or accident, or relationship that has failed in a particularly painful way (abuse, alcohol, etc.). When things like this happen and the child truly has nowhere else to go, few parents are going to say no to moving back in—for a little while.

Before accepting an adult child back, be sure the reasons are truly valid. If their moving back is merely a convenience meant to save them money they don't want to spend, put on the brakes. The remedy is hard work, maybe a second job, and facing up to the realities and responsibilities of adulthood.

When allowing a child to move home, even if they are in their 20s or 30s or older, house rules are in order. It's still your house and the parents are in charge. Make it clear what is and is not allowed. A curfew is not unreasonable. Knowing when they will be home means being able to sleep through the night without worrying about them or being awakened when they come in at 3 A.M. Other rules, such as no overnight guests or sexual activity, asking friends to not call late at night, and so on will also need to be discussed and put in place. Also agree on rent and expenses if they are able to afford anything at all.

You'll also want to reinforce your privacy. Reestablish boundaries regarding your bedroom and even other areas of the house. They need to stay out of your stuff. Make it clear that once you go to your bedroom in the evening and close the door you expect to not be disturbed. What you do behind that closed door is none of their business (well, you probably won't need to point that out to your adult children, but who knows?).

For Her

It is most likely mom who will be approached by a child wanting to come back home. Since your children have such a soft place in your heart, they've got you pegged as a soft touch. Before you give your child any indication of what you may be thinking, make it clear you need to talk to your husband before any decision can be rendered. Dads generally scrutinize things from a whole different perspective. You each will see things the other will miss. Together you can make the best decision for both your child and yourselves. Allowing a child to move back may not be in his or her best interests and your husband may recognize that before you do.

While the kids are back in the house you'll need to go back to the old cautions of always being covered when walking around the house, and knocking before entering any shared bathroom. The same would apply to the returning kids.

To preserve some of your new found sexual freedom, it may be a good idea to pre-arrange a date night when you ask your adult child to not come home before a certain time. You may just want to put them or yourselves up in a hotel room now and then. Do what you have to do to keep those flames of passion burning!

When the Kids Won't Leave

What do you do if the kids have either moved back in and won't leave, or have just never left after finishing college? Each situation is unique, but most kids need to get out on their own when they reach their mid- to late twenties. If they're still hanging around, you need to take a look at why.

Are they afraid to move out or just too lazy? Are you making it too easy for them to stay? Do you or your spouse have issues about letting go?

Life has stages and each stage has its special rewards. When the kids grow up, it's time for the empty-nest stage. You'll miss them, for sure, but you'll also be rewarded by watching them succeed in life all on their own. You'll enjoy the reward of new opportunities for intimacy with your spouse with an added dimension of age and wisdom. You'll enjoy the reward of gaining grandchildren.

Your adult children will enjoy the reward of proving themselves and relishing their accomplishments. They will enjoy the reward of pursuing careers, starting their own families, and living out their faith in a more dynamic way.

If you aren't helping your adult children to leave you need to question your motives. Who are they staying for? Why are they there? Who needs who? How unhealthy is the arrangement? Does the marriage need the adult child there to survive? (This is a really toxic situation.)

When the kids won't leave, everyone misses out. You may need to see a therapist or your pastor to deal with whatever the issues are, but don't just let the situation coast. Odds are that, even if they are unspoken, you and your spouse are feeling tension about the situation, and tension has a negative impact on your sex life and marriage.

If you are the only one complaining about this arrangement and your spouse refuses to go and see your pastor or a therapist, go alone. You are probably needing a lot of support and understanding.

Dr. Truth

Remember Genesis? The part about a man leaving his father and mother? This is a necessary part of life. It's the way God ordained things. Eventually we must all grow up and leave home. The Lord was probably as concerned about the well-being of the father and the mother as he was of the man! When our kids leave home we have the opportunity to rekindle the sparks of marriage. Continue to invest in your marriage—this may be the most pleasant and pleasurable part of your life.

Facing Up to Problems

No one is perfect. Being human in a sinful world means having problems, challenges, wounds, and issues. Most are manageable or fixable with a little effort. A few are virtually negligible and easily tolerated. Some, however, can be huge and debilitating if left unattended. With the help of the Holy Spirit, and in some instances the support of a pastor or therapist, even the biggest problems can be knocked down to size.

This chapter addresses serious emotional dysfunction, physical abuse, and addictions—problems that should never be ignored. An emotionally dysfunctional relationship isn't a relationship with a few little problems—it's one where one or both parties have some serious emotional/mental issues or brokenness that require individual attention. Physical abuse often goes unmentioned in the church, but it is a sin like any other. There are spouses who suffer in silence and fear. This is not what the Lord wants for anybody, and any marriage that exists with physical violence is not glorifying God. Secret addictions poison marriages. They need to be exposed and dealt with, the sooner the better. The truth is what we must adhere to. Secrecy is the cancer of the soul.

Emotional Dysfunction

Probably the most prevalent and multi-faceted problems couples will confront are their individual and joint emotional issues.

Even if your parents were for the most part healthy, loving, and supportive, emotional dysfunction on some level could still exist.

Perhaps your mother was subtly overbearing or your father was sometimes emotionally distant. The parents of most baby boomers believed that it was inappropriate for a father to show physical affection as his children got older. It wasn't the manly thing to do with a boy, and it was improper with a girl. The kids ended up confused and feeling rejected.

It was also not uncommon for Christian parents to limit the discussion of sex in the household and not explain why. This created the unspoken subtext that somehow all sex was bad or dirty.

Carrying Our Emotional Baggage

Emotional baggage? Who needs it? We'd all like to get through life without it, wouldn't we? The fact is, there is no perfect life, not for anyone.

All of us are affected by the way we were raised. We are affected by the roles our parents taught us (or didn't), the values they taught us (or didn't), the way they treated each other (good or bad), the way they used alcohol (or abused it), the way they affirmed us (or didn't), the work ethic they modeled to us (or didn't), the way they communicated with each other (or didn't), the way they disciplined us (or didn't), the way they rewarded our efforts (or didn't), and the list goes on.

In addition to how we were raised in our families is the dimension of hurts and pains occurring outside our families. A serious illness of a loved one, emotional trauma in the school yard, sexual abuse and incest, being victimized by a crime, and many other things can leave us emotionally wounded in such a way as to affect our marriages.

One thing we know about emotional health is that we tend to marry people whose emotional health is similar to our own. Emotionally healthy people tend to marry emotionally healthy people. Emotionally unhealthy people tend to marry emotionally unhealthy people.

Imagine a teeter-totter, a man on one end, a woman on the other. The farther from the center they sit, the more exaggerated their motion. But the closer to the center they sit, the more calm their motion. Men and women who are relatively "well-balanced" (so to speak) tend to sit closer to the center of their emotional teeter-totter. Those with some level of dysfunction tend to sit farther apart, toward the ends of the teeter-totter—and experience the pronounced highs and lows of the dysfunctional couple.

This is good news to those who are relatively healthy, bad news for those who are more dysfunctional. Couples who are relatively healthy go into marriage and have the emotional strength to make all of the little adjustments that are necessary to live harmoniously with little if any therapeutic intervention.

Even though, for some couples, it may look as though one person is healthy and the other is unhealthy, the dysfunction of the one who looks healthy is not always noticed. For example, there are marriages where either the husband or wife is obviously troubled and their spouse looks like a saint. The saint is probably in the role of an enabler who, instead of caring for their own needs, focuses their life around the unhealthy mate. Perhaps they have a Messiah-complex or a martyr complex. Perhaps they are focusing on their mate's emotional pain as a way of avoiding their own.

Dealing with Dysfunction

Couples where both husband and wife have more serious personal dysfunction can have a tough time making the necessary marital adjustments; instead, the marriage may become more and more painful and bitter. In these situations, each person is trying so hard to maintain their own sense of themselves that they will try to hold on to as much personal power as they can. The couple can begin to play one power game after another. One of three scenarios can ensue: they can both try to exert obvious power through verbal or physical fighting; both can use covert power by nonverbal actions and behaviors to out-do the other one or control them; or one of them may try to exert overt power while the other counters with covert power. Unfortunately for these couples, sex can become just one more way to maintain power in the relationship.

When sexual intimacy is used as part of the power games between the couple it can be toxic. The couple may be avoiding sex altogether or there may be a sexual aggressor (it could be the husband or the wife). Sometimes there may be a sexual victim who gives in to sex to avoid the other person's anger or to get them to finally leave them alone for a while (it could be the husband or the wife).

Couples with the greatest sexual dysfunction are those with the greatest emotional dysfunction. When this is the case, personal counseling as well as marital counseling are required.

If your marriage is troubled, be encouraged. Through Christ Jesus, there is healing available to all who seek him with their whole heart. Jesus came for those who were hurting and needy. It may take a large investment of your time, energy, and money to get your marriage to a healthy state, but it is possible when both of you are willing and have open hearts and soft spirits.

Physical Abuse

If there is physical abuse in your marriage there are two things going on: one is complete disrespect of the person being hurt, and the other is total insecurity in the one doing the hurting. There can be no equitable sexual intimacy when there is physical abuse in your marriage.

Do not be deceived if the hitting is occurring occasionally. Whether it is once a year or once a month doesn't matter. It is a sign of great problems. Do not make excuses for the one doing the hurting. Those who abuse their spouses increase the frequency of attacks over the years and the attacks become more and more damaging (and can become life threatening).

After an abusive episode, the abusing spouse usually attempts to make amends, do sweet and loving things for the one they hurt, promise never to do it again, ask forgiveness, appear repentant, and so on. Do not be deceived. Such displays are part of the cycle of physical abuse. There can be no healthy marriage unless the abuser gets help. If this cycle describes your marriage, please consult a professional who specifically works in the area of domestic violence and anger management. Let the spiritual authorities in your church know whom can then provide spiritual discipline and require true repentance.

For Her

Please, if you are in an abusive marriage, seek help. The Lord loves you and cares about you so much. Any man who is hurting his wife is not living a Christ-centered life (even if it looks like it on the surface). Women are specifically told in the Bible that they are not obligated to stay with a man who is not living for the Lord. (1 Corinthians 7:15) If he is abusive to you he's not living for the Lord. Period.

The Lord does not expect any innocent person to put him- or herself in harm's way. It is not ungodly to protect yourself and your children from physical danger even when it is your spouse who puts you at risk. This type of situation can't be ignored, and it won't get better without serious, long-term intervention with mental health specialists.

For Him

There are men who are abused by their wives. It is even harder for them to seek help because of embarrassment and the feeling that they are weak and unmasculine. There are women who attack their husbands and bruise them. There are women who are so vicious mentally and verbally that they traumatize and torment their husbands with their mouths. Abuse is abuse.

Sex in a marriage where physical abuse exists can be varied. When the abusive spouse is in the "sucking up" stage, showering you with gifts and apologies, the sex might be great. However, if he is in the battering stage you might be sexually assaulted or raped. Yes, all nonconsensual sex is sexual assault. Marriage is not a license for nonconsensual sex. Just because you married him doesn't give him license to use your body whenever and however he pleases. Rape is not love, it is control. God is not glorified when your husband sins against you or when you passively accept the sin against you.

Addiction Issues

Addiction is a compulsive physiological or psychological need for a substance or behavior. It is a habit out of control. You can become addicted to almost anything. Some addictions involve something good that's become harmful (such as an addiction to food), or something that is inherently harmful that has become a compulsion (such as illegal drugs). Addictions can include food, pornography, alcohol, illegal and legal drugs, smoking, gambling, spending, sex, the Internet, TV, coffee, sugar, exercise, and more.

Whatever the addiction, it will eventually affect your marriage. It is inevitable since every addiction, no matter how manageable it seems at first, will escalate out of control if left untreated. Out-of-control addictions can lead to serious illness, divorce, injury, incarceration, and even death.

Certain addictions will more directly affect your sex life than others. Someone continually indulging in pornography and masturbation will generally have a much lower interest in normal sexual relations with his or her spouse. Abusing legal or illegal drugs can leave a person disinterested or physically unable to have sex, or drive a person to obsessive violent sex.

Beyond the physical and emotional consequences of addictions, there are the spiritual consequences. A Christian caught up in any addictive behavior is going to be torn between serving Christ and serving their craving.

Whenever one person in a relationship has an addiction, most of the time, the person they are in a relationship with is codependent. You may be unconsciously aiding and abetting your spouse's addiction or you may have tried to help them and come to the end of your rope. You may want to contact local chapters of Alcoholics Anonymous or Narcotics Anonymous for further information on codependency.

Codependent relationships perpetuate an addiction. If you feel that you have to protect your partner from exposure or keep the troubling behaviors secret, please know, "Secrecy is the cancer of your soul."

Word from the Wise

"But don't be afraid of those who threaten you. For the time is coming when everything will be revealed; all that is secret will be made public." (Matthew 10: 26)

Fear of telling someone what is really happening in your house is the first indication that you *must* tell and get help. The Lord never endorsed keeping sin, pain, and hurt secret.

Getting Help

How does one go about getting help? Good question. As with any profession there are people with more or less training, more or less experience, specializations that may or may not apply, and so on. The same holds true for mental health professionals.

When we mention that there are times and circumstances where a professional should probably be engaged, what we have in mind is someone with specialized training.

There are therapists who specialize in "marriage and family therapy." There are lots of people who might print in their telephone ad, their brochures, or on their business cards that they do marriage counseling/therapy and/or family counseling/therapy. Some states and provinces have licensing for marriage and family therapists and some don't. The licensing authority may or may not require them to specifically have a degree in marriage and family therapy. There are many ways to find out if a therapist is well trained specifically in marriage and family therapy.

The American Association of Marriage and Family Therapy (www.aamft.org) has a listing on its website of all of the Clinical Members of AAMFT. All of these people have advanced training in working with couples and families.

Besides Clinical Members of AAMFT there are Associate and Affiliate Members. These people aren't allowed to be listed on the AAMFT website. This doesn't mean they aren't well trained, only that they may not quite have finished their supervision hours since they finished their training. If you have the name of a therapist, call the state or provincial arm of the AAMFT (e.g., Indiana Association of Marriage and Family Therapy, Alberta Association of Marriage and Family Therapy) and ask if the person you know of is an Associate or Affiliate Member. Of course, you could just ask the therapist personally.

The AAMFT accredits Master's degrees and Doctoral degrees that meet their training standards. Make some calls and try to find out who in your area has taken their training at an AAMFT Accredited School. You can ask the therapist directly about this. Because of the licensing in different jurisdictions, the AAMFT graduate might be licensed as a psychologist or mental health counselor, which would give you no indication of the AAMFT training. These are questions you need to ask.

Aside from marriage and family therapists, there are many psychologists and counselors you could see. Many will not have taken a single class in their training on marriage counseling or family counseling. And one class of this subject is nothing like taking a full training program for two or three years in this specialized area. You can ask the therapist specifically if they have had classes in family systems and the marital dyad.

After you find out the person's training you can ask how long they have been working in this profession. It's perfectly okay to ask as many questions as you need to including questions about their level of experience.

Word from the Wise

"... if another Christian is overcome by some sin, you who are godly should gently and humbly help that person back onto the right path. And be careful not to fall into the same temptation yourself. Share each other's troubles and problems, and in this way obey the law of Christ." (Galatians 6:1-2)

We need to bear our burdens with each other, not keep them to ourselves. As a community of faith we need to deal with sin, with hurt, with pain. As we heal in Christ's love and with his resources we become a witness to the world of his healing power.

Of course, word of mouth is highly important in finding a therapist. Try to find someone who will make a recommendation for you based on their personal knowledge of the therapist and their effectiveness. Make sure that at least his or her values and theories align well with your Christian beliefs.

If your personal issues predate the marriage, your range of options increases. Your issues may or may not involve the family you grew up in and you may not need someone with this specialized training. If you were a sexual abuse victim you need to look for someone who has specialized in abuse recovery. If you were a physical abuse victim ask questions of the therapist to find out if they have previously worked with people who have been hurt like you have. Did the therapist take any training in domestic violence or trauma recovery? Is alcoholism a problem for you? You need to see someone who is specially trained in chemical dependency.

The point is, you have the right to make these inquiries before you go to see the therapist. If a therapist has never done abuse recovery work before, therapy will be much longer for you. This is because the therapist will be learning how to treat abuse issues alongside of working with you.

Try to make sure that you see a licensed mental health professional when possible but do ask the questions. There are many people who became licensed because of "grandfathering." This means that they were doing counseling work (not necessarily with adequate training) long before the jurisdiction brought in licensing. They were all given an opportunity to license without taking a licensing exam, and many of them without ever having their work supervised. This is scary for the consumer; a person may have been licensed or in the profession a long time but have inadequate training. If such a person has a good reputation for successfully treating people, go and see them. Otherwise, feel free to ask about the courses, classes, workshops, and training seminars that they have taken related to the area of expertise you need.

Dr. Truth

Above all you ought to be comfortable with the therapist and feel a good connection with them right from the beginning. You will find the following statement in the intake forms I give to my new clients: "All therapists recognize the need for there to be a good client-therapist 'fit' for successful counseling to take place. I may not be the person to best work with you." No matter how good the therapist is and what kind of reputation they have, if the client doesn't connect with the therapist, it's time to find someone else because your resistance will be too high.

Part

4

A Few Important Details

What happens outside your bedroom will have a direct effect on what happens in your bedroom, or wherever else you choose to make love. Issues of trust, respect, privacy, and more need to be discussed openly. Matters of faith are important as well. The healthier your faith in God, the better your sex life and marriage will be.

Intimacy is the glue that keeps marriages together for better and for worse, in sickness and in health, in youth and in old age. As you grow old together, your sex life can still be vital and young!

Privacy Is Healthy

Just because you're married does not mean that you give up all of your privacy, or that you have the right to pry into every tiny little corner of your spouse's life, thoughts, and stuff. Allowing each other privacy is healthy. It encourages and builds trust and respect.

Being Alone Is a Good Thing

In the early days of love the thought of having to be apart seems horrendous. You feel as if you want to be in the arms of your beloved 24 hours a day, 7 days a week. Or at least within earshot and eyesight of them. Now that you've found your one true soul mate, so you reason, why would you ever want to let him or her out of your sight even for a short while?

Why? Because it's normal. Remember the song by The Police, "Every Breath You Take"? Sting's voice is wonderful and the melody is sweet and seductive. However, the words are actually alarming. It's more a stalker's anthem than a love song. In fact, many pop songs contain lyrics that imply obsession and possessiveness rather than true love.

Normal healthy relationships require periods where the couple is apart. Healthy individuals need time alone, especially if they're introverts (people energized by solitude and inner dialogue) rather than extroverts (people energized by interactions with other people). Alone time, or down time, is an opportunity to recharge.

Taking time for yourself without having to be bothered by interruptions, demands, or expectations from another helps you maintain your identity and sanity, as well as gives you time to nurture your personal relationship with God.

Allowing each other regular periods of being alone will also enhance your times together. Have you ever heard the old adage, absence makes the heart grow fonder? There is real truth there. Before marriage, you and your spouse had separate identities. Those identities follow you into marriage. While oneness does occur, becoming one does not mean the obliteration of individual personalities. Before marriage there were things you both enjoyed doing together, and there were things you enjoyed doing alone that the other did not care for. This is not a bad thing.

In marriage, there will be negotiation as to what you do together, and you will both learn to enjoy or at least tolerate doing together some of the things you don't enjoy personally. Insisting that you both do everything together and that you spend every free moment together will most likely lead to resentment and problems.

If you are anxious when you are not with your spouse, there are issues related to insecurity, fear, and the like that you need to explore with a counselor. On the same hand, if you never want to spend any time with your spouse, there are intimacy and other issues you will need to explore with a counselor. Marriage and oneness involves a balancing of time together and time apart. You will necessarily spend less time alone after marriage, but you both will still need some alone time.

Word from the Wise

"Afterward he went up into the hills by himself to pray. Night fell while he was there alone." (Matthew 14:23)

Jesus regularly went off, away from his disciples and everyone else, to be alone. Often he used this time to pray and talk with God. Each time he came back renewed and refreshed, better able to minister to others.

Ways to work these times in can be very simple. Perhaps you take turns doing the grocery shopping, giving one spouse a couple of hours at home. On the way home from work, stop for a cup of coffee and spend a few minutes by yourself. If you have kids, take turns taking the kids out to a movie or other activity from time to time. Be creative.

Recognize, too, that one of you may need a little more alone time than the other. This is not unusual. If your spouse is very introverted, having to deal with people at the office can be draining for them. They may need an hour to themselves every night after work to regroup, plus a bigger chunk of time on the weekends. During the week, it could be as simple as leaving them alone in the bedroom or some other area of the house for an hour, and keeping the kids away from them. Giving them this time will allow your introverted spouse to be reenergized to focus on you. Both of you benefit.

If both you and your spouse are introverts you will both know that you need time alone to reenergize. If one of you is an extrovert and the other is an introvert, there will be negotiations that will need to occur. The danger with the two of you is that one of you thinks you are "right" and the other "wrong" when really it is personality style and temperament that are different. In the introvert-extrovert marriage the extrovert must allow the introvert their space but the introvert cannot take advantage of this and use it to avoid the extrovert. The introvert must commit himself or herself to spending time talking with the extrovert. Also, the extrovert must find other ways to get their needs met because their introverted spouse will never be able to talk with them as much as they would like. They need a few good extroverted friends to spend a few talking hours with now and then.

The craziest of all couples are those with two extroverts. Each person ends up heavily involved at work and in social contacts and outings. Extroverts get very involved in community, school, and church. When there are two in the marriage there isn't anybody pulling in the reigns. Extroverts really need to work to find time for each other because they get so busy and caught up in so many things that they can literally forget to spend time nurturing their marriage.

The extreme extrovert experiences no need to be alone. They don't seem to understand that everyone else in the world doesn't tick the same way they do. They can be seen as very intrusive and demanding both inside marriage and outside marriage. The usual extrovert has an appreciation that other people need alone time. The extreme extrovert may be running from himself or herself and may well need to spend time alone to discover what they are running from. One sign of a healthy person is that they can be alone for a while and be okay (peaceful, relaxed, and calm).

Protecting Each Other's Privacy

We all have bits and pieces of our lives we would rather not have disclosed. It could be some dumb embarrassing thing you did as a child or a stupid mistake you made as an adult. In our families, we rely on parents and siblings to help us protect our privacy. It's important to know that we have a safe place where we can be ourselves and share secrets without being exposed.

As adults on your own, protecting your privacy is simpler. As long as you don't spill the beans about yourself, your secrets are safe with you. You determine how much of yourself you will share with others. You decide who you will invite into your home or apartment. You decide with whom you will discuss medical issues, romantic interests, and spiritual questions, as well as how much about these and other areas you will open up to them.

As a married couple, your responsibility increases. You will open up to your spouse more of your life than you have ever opened to anyone else. What you share with your spouse and what they share with you, is for you and your spouse, not for others. This includes children, parents, best friends, relatives, and, well, others.

Being sensitive in this area is critical. Your spouse may share things with you that for them are really private, hard to share details and bits of information. You, however, may not view this type of information the same way, thinking this is the stuff of general knowledge. Women tend to share far more among themselves than men do. It's not uncommon for a man to share something with his wife that he does not want others to know about, only to have his wife think nothing of telling her best friend. He's devastated and she wonders what the big deal is. If the situation were reversed, she would know what the big deal was.

For Him

Never share any details of your sex life with the guys. It's none of their business and it is demeaning to your wife. Given the rampant nature of a man's imagination, sharing sexual intimacies with your guy friends is practically inviting them into your bedroom. Confiding issues to one trusted Christian best friend who you know will maintain a confidence is one thing. Talking about your bedroom exploits in a group of guys is just wrong. Honor your wife by protecting her privacy just as you want her to protect yours.

The key is, when in doubt, keep it to yourself. What you and your spouse say to each other in private is, generally, no one else's business. Unless you have both clearly agreed that information can be shared, don't share it. Protect each other's privacy. Create in your marriage an absolutely safe haven for each other.

Some things you will know you shouldn't share—like the sexual secrets your spouse shares with you. Other things you share may not seem to be private to you at all, like talking about the kids. To cover all the bases it's a good idea when you share something you know you want to keep between the two of you to make a point to tell your spouse that you want this kept between the two of you. It's better safe than sorry.

For Her

Women share way more intimate details of their lives with their girlfriends than men. Men can be down right shocked to know what women talk about. Be careful. Protect your husband. Unless you are concerned about some serious deviation or abuse, don't share your husband's personal information with your girlfriends. This doesn't mean you can't talk about having had a great night of sex with your husband though and how sore you are as a result! Gals like to laugh about that kind of stuff.

For women it can be a real hoot to tell your friend what a great double or triple orgasm night you had. That's one thing. It's quite another to give any actual details that include the sexual behaviors or actions of either your husband or yourself. While one type of storytelling can be okay for women to speak of, there is a limit. Make sure you don't disgrace your husband or talk about him in a negative light.

Giving Each Other Space

Privacy is one thing, space is another. For some reason, women always seem to need so much more than men, at least when it comes to closet space! The reality is, you both need your space, or spaces, around the house. These are areas where you keep your stuff, neatly, the way you want it. For example, the table next to your chair, your side of the sink, mostly her kitchen and mostly his garage, his office and her office, etc.

For Her

Do you want your husband to love to come to bed with you? Take the time to find out what is important to him in terms of personal time and personal space in the house. Ask him how you can protect him sexually. Listen to him and make some adjustments. The investment will come back to you.

Allow each other these spaces. Keep them tidy and clean (especially if they're semi-public areas like the living room or family room), but keep them the way you want them. Then respect each other's spaces and protect them from others (a.k.a. the kids!).

When it comes to the closet, be fair. Women usually do need a little more space than men do. Yet it isn't unusual for both to hold onto clothing that they no longer wear or that no longer fits. Clean the closet out regularly and give the stuff to Goodwill or the Salvation Army. Don't hog closet space you don't really need. Make accommodations for one another to keep clothing stored neatly.

Speaking of closets, the old-fashioned expression "prayer closet" should be an important part of your private life. Get quiet time every day by retreating to a private space where you and the Lord can commune. You'll treat your spouse much better after spending time in God's presence.

Staying Out of Each Other's Stuff

There are few situations more challenging than having an "a-place-for-everything-and-everything-in-its-place" person and a "file-by-pile-and-leave-it-where-it-lands" person try to live together. Add to this volatile mix a lack of respect for each other's stuff and you've got the ingredients for World War III. Compromise and negotiation rather than war are the way to go.

Being married means you will share pretty much everything at some point. But it doesn't mean that you are free to rummage through each other's bureau drawers whenever the urge strikes. It's important to show each other common courtesy as much as possible, especially early on in a marriage. Access, whether to stuff or thoughts, is something to be allowed rather than demanded.

While from time to time, you may need to search through your spouse's things because you know they've stashed the family camera somewhere, it's best to do it with permission as often as possible. If the situation does not allow time for seeking permission, then you need to let them know what's been done as soon as possible after the fact.

Sharing openly with each other can happen with consideration and respect. Keeping your hands off his or her stuff is particularly important around gift-giving times. If Christmas is coming or a birthday or anniversary is nearing, don't go snooping. If your husband comes home from a shopping trip, don't demand that he open his packages up for your inspection. If you later come across one of those packages stashed in a corner, don't touch it and don't ask about it. If the gift-giving occasion comes and goes and the mystery package is still in its hiding place, mention it to your spouse in passing, letting them know you just happened to notice it while cleaning or looking for something else.

However, there may be an exception to the no-snooping policy. If your spouse is frequently hiding things or being secretive, something else may be going on. View their behavior in context of other things you know to be going on with them. Probe gently and lovingly. Pray for guidance and discernment. If you come across hidden drugs,

Dr. Truth

Take the time to talk with each other about privacy and space issues. You may learn a few new things from each other. Talk about how the two of you can balance these things so that you both feel satisfied with the plan. The safer you both feel, the more free you will be sexually.

alcohol, pornography, love letters, or anything else that causes concern, confront them gently and insist on going to counseling together.

If, however, you just feel compelled to search through your spouse's belongings or read their private journal whenever they're not around or grill them about everything they're doing or thinking, you may have some trust and other issues to deal with. Seeing a counselor would be a good idea. Being overly possessive of the one you love is a good way to push them away.

Issues of space and privacy might not quickly appear to have anything to do with sexual intimacy. Remember sexual interest and excitement develops all day long, not just at bedtime. Sexual interest depends on many things, respect and privacy being two of those things. When we know that our spouse is guarding our sexuality and protecting our marriage bed, there is so much more freedom to become a passionate, sensual lover with your spouse. Who wants to disclose themselves in bed if their spouse is "disclothing" them out of bed?

We need to establish emotional safety with each other. Emotional safety is negatively impacted by being too intrusive, not allowing your spouse to have the emotional and physical space they need, not guarding intimate knowledge of them, and invading their private areas of the house. Negative impacts to emotional safety will leave your spouse less interested in sharing the intimate part of themselves with you.

 Word from the Wise

"Don't give what is holy to unholy people. Don't give pearls to swine! They will trample the pearls, then turn and attack you." (Matthew 7:6)

Among other interpretations, your pearls can be seen as private intimate pieces of information that you have about yourself and your spouse which includes your sexual history and your sex life. You can never be absolutely sure what another person will do with your pearls. But in a Christ-centered marriage, your pearls will be protected, grow, and become more valuable.

Chapter 18

Sharing Stuff Is Fun

Newlyweds often don't have a lot of individual belongings, and most of what's acquired happens in the marriage. In this case determining what belongs to who is not as much of an issue but there can be exceptions. Those who have been divorced and are remarrying will have more of a challenge in this area. Often, a house, cars, and other significant property are involved.

His Stuff, Her Stuff, Our Stuff

As stated in Chapter 17, it's a good thing to respect each other's stuff and privacy. Yet, as was mentioned, in marriage, at some point, you will pretty much share everything to some extent.

For first time newlyweds, it's usually pretty obvious who brought what into the marriage. His possessions often scream "bachelor pad" and hers "princess house." It is not unusual for both to decide to replace the old with new stuff purchased together, better reflecting their maturity and position in life.

Those who are getting married again may have a few more issues regarding sharing. Particularly if in a prior marriage one or the other was the "dumped" spouse or if a former spouse resisted splitting up the possessions, even withholding things unfairly. What was successfully claimed from the old marriage or what has been gained since may carry with it a very strong sense of ownership. Sharing won't be easy.

Often, it isn't until a couple is remarried and living together that these issues surface. It happens when one wants to use something else that "belongs" to the other and holds special meaning. Sometimes the more valuable the item, the bigger the issue. Just agreeing where something will be placed in the house can require a long discussion. Referring to any of these things as "ours" can be dangerous!

How can these issues be resolved? Usually they resolve themselves over time and that's the key. If you respect each other's "possessiveness" in the beginning, and ask permission to use what belongs to the other, and take care of what belongs to the other, eventually what's his or hers will eventually become ours.

If your spouse brought his or her favorite chair into the marriage, don't expect that you'll get to share that! That's their chair. Many people end up with favorite chairs and making an issue out of something like that is useless. You can't cut it in half and you will never be welcome to it. One way we respect each other is to let the other person have their stuff. If we have much of a need to possess our spouse's stuff, that may be a sign of trouble. The longer you're married the less of an issue it will be. Also, the longer you're married, the more stuff you'll purchase together and this won't be an issue.

If ownership issues cause ongoing tension and arguments, you both need to go to a therapist to work it out. Don't let stuff get in the way of your marriage. It's better you let them have their stuff than get in a fight about it. "Our stuff" develops over years, not overnight.

Word from the Wise

"I would never have known that coveting is wrong if the law had not said, 'Do not covet.' But sin took advantage of this law and aroused all kinds of forbidden desires within me! If there were no law, sin would not have that power." (Romans 7:7-8)

To preoccupy yourself with your spouse's possessions can be sinful. If this becomes a preoccupation for you, repentance may be in order. The Lord does not want you to have this sort of sin in your heart. As you grow more and more into your married life, sharing will develop naturally. Let it be so.

There is a certain danger for a marriage where "our stuff" never develops. Marriage is a joint venture. If you are married for the first time and have trouble sharing earned income and resources acquired during the marriage with your spouse, there is a problem. You may be protecting yourself in anticipation of possible divorce while at the same time sabotaging the development of the marriage so that it doesn't come to divorce. If you are married for the first time and you or your spouse is not sharing their income and resources within the marriage, or keeping separate accounts or secret accounts, it's an issue. You may be creating a self-fulfilling prophecy. Get to a therapist.

If you are remarried you're aware of the pain of divorce and how possessions can be used in a power struggle as you have one more fight together, the fight of divorce. It is true that what you bring into the marriage is yours, unless you commingle it in your new marriage. You may be cautious and that is totally understandable. You and your spouse may both go through a time of testing to make sure that this marriage will survive before you really share anything valuable that you have. You may need to go through a period where you put equal amounts into the marriage to keep it equitable. Over the first several years this should dissolve as an issue. While you may still keep separate your savings or investments, what you are acquiring while married needs to be shared.

Remarried people would do well to get a legal consultation about their investments before or right after they remarry. While you may be very willing to share with your spouse, if your spouse dies without a will, his or her children may have an entitlement to that which was commingled, that which was previously only yours. Remarried people need to recognize that they need to consider their own children in their estate planning and make provisions for part of their estate to go directly to them. Planning your estate with your children in mind does not undermine your second marriage. It attempts to strike a balance between the children of your first marriage, perhaps children of your second marriage, and your spouse. It's not easy but it's something every remarried person needs to deal with.

Being Together

You won't want to do everything together, but it's a good idea to do something together. Early in a marriage, this usually isn't a problem. Unless you're both at work, you're both together setting up your new household. As the marriage continues, and especially as children come along, being together gets a little more challenging. You'll need to make time just to be alone with each other, as well as making time for having sex.

That's right, being together isn't just about having sex. It's about talking to one another, listening to one another, and just being in one another's presence.

Easy ways to accomplish this would include shopping together, running errands together, or taking a walk around the block together. Maybe it's just sitting on the couch in front of the fireplace for a few minutes after the kids are in bed.

Reading while together, reading to each other, doing a daily devotional together, listening to music together, all of these activities provide times to connect. Take a Sunday afternoon drive to new place or explore a museum or a botanical garden.

Some couples find a hobby to do together just to have one thing they do together because otherwise their interests are so different. Bird watching, star gazing, photography, mountain climbing, hang gliding, and gardening are all activities that a couple can choose to do together just so that they do something together.

These are moments to connect with each other and recapture the early days of romance. Remember when it was so urgent and just enough to sit with your beloved, quietly, leaning up against them? It can still be good even after you've been married for several years.

Continuing to pay attention to the needs of the marriage will always be important. Some people get divorced because they say they "grew apart." What the heck is that? If you feel like you and your spouse are growing apart it's time to take action and work to reverse that trend.

> **For Him**
>
> Men tend to be a tad more competitive than women, and this extends to their stuff. The more that's "his" the bigger man he is, is the thought. Not necessarily. In marriage, "his and hers" is more about equally sharing and not divvying up the goods.

Marriages take time and attention. There are three entities in your house: the husband, the wife, and the marriage. You have to recognize that "the marriage" has its own life. The marriage needs both of you to make decisions in the same direction in order for it to exist. The marriage can't exist without you—both of you. Being together nurtures the marriage. When the marriage is nurtured, intimacy remains alive and well. The older we get, the more we value intimacy whether sex is involved or not. Intimacy becomes much more about being together as we age.

Building Traditions

Strong families are built on strong traditions. You and your spouse should be establishing and reinforcing traditions in your new family even if it's just the two of you.

Traditions include such things as how you worship, what you eat for your main Christmas meal, who you invite for Thanksgiving, how much you spend on each other for anniversary gifts, and more. Traditions provide points of stability and help build meaning into our lives.

Your traditions can be taken in part or in whole from traditions you grew up with and blended with those of your spouse. Making your own traditions together is also a good way to replace those from either family that you never cared for.

If you are remarrying and you have children, you will want to preserve traditions your kids are familiar with, while at the same time creating new ones.

Because you each had your own traditions before your marriage you may walk into traditional holidays planning to just do things the way your family did or the way you did them in your previous marriage. You may unknowingly be trampling over your spouse. Your spouse may end up feeling totally left out of everything that just took place and feel like they were just shuffled in with the rest of the deck. These types of things may catch you both off guard in the first year of marriage. Before (and if not, after) each holiday talk about what you anticipate happening on that day. Share with each other what you'd like to see happen and how you can both put parts of yourself into how that day develops.

While building traditions can take some work and some conversation, how traditions are built has to be about both of you, not just about one of you. If one of you is a little more forthright and the other is a little more laid back, make sure the laid-back person offers their preferences before final decisions are made. Sometimes the laid-back person who appears not to care will silently be upset or unhappy that all these things happen the way you want them and they don't feel you will really listen to them anyway. They could be looking laid back because they don't think they have a chance. Do you love your laid-back spouse, do you value their input? Then make sure you listen to them and don't make unilateral decisions.

 ### For Her

Women tend to be a little more verbal than men. Make sure you consider your husband's thoughts, his preferences and especially, the things that he really doesn't like. Make sure his agreement is his agreement, not just acquiescence! When he knows you really do value his input and opinion he'll feel respected. You can win the little battle and lose the war by doing it just your way.

Establishing Acceptable Together Behaviors

Every individual is, in a sense, an entire unique culture. Even growing up in a family, you have likes and dislikes that are different from your parents and siblings. You have your quirks and preferences, and each member of your family has theirs.

A family also, taken as a whole, is a unique mini-culture compared to every other family. What is accepted behavior in your family may be the height of rudeness in another.

If you and your spouse are childhood friends and grew up on the same block, you will still encounter differences over what is and what is not acceptable behavior. If you and your spouse are from different parts of the same country, the differences may be more pronounced. If you're from different countries or different ethnic backgrounds, the challenges get more complex.

Word from the Wise

"This should be your ambition: to live a quiet life, minding your own business and working with your hands, just as we commanded you before. As a result, people who are not Christians will respect the way you live ..." (Thessalonians 4:11-12)

In order to live together in peace, you will need to compromise and negotiate as to what you can live with when you are together. It's all tied to courtesy and respect for one another.

Part of living together in peace is about agreeing on the simple things, the everyday things. Peace is not gained so much in the big things as in all the little nitpicky things in life. We generally pick a spouse who agrees with us on the big things, but what makes or breaks a marriage is not the underlying values of life a person has, but how they deal with living together every day.

For example, you could agree that it's okay to burp when sitting in the family room as long as the culprit says, "Excuse me." Yes, even burping may need to be discussed.

At the dinner table, we agree to pray before we eat each meal. Or maybe we just pray before we eat the dinner meal. Do we pray before every meal in a restaurant or not? When asking for something to be passed at the table do we reinforce saying please and thank you? How do we teach our kids manners and respect? Do we make sure we thank the cook for his or her meal?

When lounging around the house, do we agree that it is never appropriate to be clad only in your underwear? Do we agree that wearing a housecoat is necessary when the kids are at home and that a nightgown or pajamas aren't enough?

Do we squeeze the toothpaste tube in the middle or from the end? Can we agree or do we each need to just have our own tube? Do we clean our hair out of the tub when we've finished our shower or bath? Do we hang up our towels after a bath or leave them in a pile on the floor? Believe it or not, these kinds of things can really get on a person's nerves and create unnecessary fights.

Why bother with these issues? Acceptable behavior for you may be considered rude behavior by your spouse. If you insist on your behavior, you will be insisting on offending your spouse. This will only foster tension and distance between you. Talking about these things, respecting the difference of opinions, and working toward compromises enhances the bond of marriage.

We ought to be able to work these things through and come to negotiated agreements. If the two of you are having trouble dealing with these everyday, mundane, nitpicky things there is more going on than meets the eye. It's more than likely there is some kind of power battle going on between you. Make that appointment with the marriage counselor.

Dr. Truth

Don't forget why you got married! You decided you wanted companionship and love, year after year, until death do you part. You and your spouse are in the process of creating a healthy, happy marriage. Both of you need to work together to deal with the small things so that you can enjoy each day together. The sooner you can resolve differences over the small things, the sooner you will be living in peace together. Where there is peace, intimacy follows.

Chapter 19

Respect Is Seductive

One of the more wrongly interpreted biblical concepts related to marriage is the idea of submission. It is sad that there are men who claim to be Christian who warp this idea to mean that they have the right to abuse their wives. There is nothing in the Bible that endorses or justifies a man abusing his wife, or his children, in any way. Abuse of any kind is wrong.

Biblical submission is not about abuse. In fact, it is at the opposite end of the spectrum. In Chapter 5 we touched on five elements that make up a good marriage—reverent submission, beneficent selflessness, mutual holiness, complete commitment, and loving respect. Here, we will expand on each of these. They are based on Ephesians 5:21-33.

Reverent Submission

Submission is a loaded term. Few people are comfortable with the idea of submitting to anyone or anything. A submissive person is thought to be weak, powerless. So when the biblical passages relating to submission are quoted, women cringe and men gloat. Both responses are wrong.

As with any segment of scripture, you can understand it fully only if you consider it in the context of the whole Bible. It's also important to understand the terms in the sense that they were being used at the time the verses were written.

What's Paul getting at with this submission thing? It's definitely not about one person lording it over another. Submission as it's being used in this and in a sister passage ("You wives must submit to your husbands, as is fitting for those who belong to the Lord. And you husbands must love your wives and never treat them harshly." Colossians 3:18-19) is not about forced compliance. It is about a choice, a humble act of the will.

 Word from the Wise

"... you husbands must give honor to your wives. Treat her with understanding as you live together. She may be weaker than you are, but she is your equal partner in God's gift of new life. If you don't treat her as you should, your prayers will not be heard." (1 Peter 3:7)

Abuse can take many forms and is never acceptable. Hurting one's spouse or children is wrong. Spouses are meant to protect one another and to protect their children against the harms that a sinful world can inflict.

It is also about choosing to submit one's self to another who is required to be loving and kind in return. It is not at all about being forced into tyrannical or harmful compliance to an abusive or hurtful situation.

For Him

Being respectful toward and considerate of your wife will be viewed as very sexy. Being a bully or hardheaded about everything is a turn-off. (It works the other way around too, ladies.)

Paul opens by stating there needs to be mutual reverent submission. The model is our individual choice to submit ourselves to Jesus Christ—an act that yields us the benefits of forgiveness of sins and eternal life, not harm.

It means to humbly revere one another equally. This cannot be demanded of only one. It is a requirement of husband and wife toward each other in a Christ-like manner. It grows out of your personal submission to the will and love of Jesus Christ and is enabled through the power of the Holy Spirit.

Beneficent Selflessness

Are you willing to die for your spouse? This isn't only about putting yourself between them and a bullet or pushing them out of the way of an oncoming car. Such sacrifice is part of what Paul means when he compares submission to Christ's giving up his life for us. Paul's words echo those of Christ, who said of love, "And here is how to measure it—the greatest love is shown when people lay down their lives for their friends" (John 15:13). Surely your spouse is your friend and more!

In marriage, there will be opportunities every day to lay down your life for each other. This means that both will need to lay down (sacrifice) aspects of their individual lives to remove barriers of intimacy within the marriage. It can be as simple as giving up always eating dinner in front of the TV to something as profound as giving up a country and culture.

Most often it's about giving up insisting on having your own way and compromising with your spouse, blending elements of what they want with what you want. Sometimes you give up what you want completely so your spouse can have what they want. Both husband and wife exhibit selflessness that yields benefits to the other, but also to the marriage as a whole, which brings things full circle to benefiting yourself.

It's one of those enigmatic truths. Persistent selfishness will eventually destroy a marriage and deny you the very thing you desired. Selflessness strengthens the marriage and gets you more of what you really want.

Mutual Holiness

Few marriages fail when true spirituality is alive in each partner. The goal is to "be holy and without fault," which can only come through a consistent walk with Christ. Each must also carefully and faithfully nurture their personal relationship with God.

One of the first things a good Christian marriage counselor will try to assess in a couple having problems is where they stand spiritually. If one or both have allowed their faith to falter, or are going through a spiritual drought, this will have an impact on the marriage.

It's not unusual for one spouse to flounder a bit spiritually while the other is hotter than ever. Even in marriage you are still an individual. Your relationship with God and your spiritual growth are personal and individual matters. You will experience highs and lows spiritually in your daily walk. It can be comforting to know that when you're feeling weak, your spouse is strong. In the course of a marriage, you will move through phases—periods where you are both together spiritually will be broken up by periods when one or the other is up or down.

Trouble comes when one or both spouses hit a spiritual low and fail to recover over an extended period of time. If you or your spouse are in an unholy funk that seems to be bottomless, scheduling time with your pastor or a Christian therapist may be a good idea. They can help you recover your spiritual bearings, and help you assess what factors may be feeding your spiritual depression.

Praying together, having devotions together, attending and being involved in church together will all contribute to a strong marital faith. If these are being neglected, be on guard.

Guard each other, too. Pray for your spouse and encourage them to holiness. Share with each other the things God is revealing in your individual study of his word. Gently caution when you see the other becoming involved in something they should not be involved in or when they are developing a coolness toward the Spirit.

Dr. Truth

Do not underestimate the power of praying together and for each other. Make it a daily routine before you get out of bed in the morning. When there is conflict between you and one or both of you feels hard-hearted toward the other, make yourselves come together, pray and ask for God's help. First we must submit ourselves before God, then we must quietly submit ourselves one to another in humility and love.

Complete Commitment

A small phrase from the most commonly used marriage vows is "forsaking all others." This does not mean that we no longer have any love or regard for other people, including our relatives. It means that our spouse is now our first focus. All others move into second place.

No other person must be allowed to come between you and your spouse—whether an old or new friend, a relative, an acquaintance, whomever. Your emotional allegiance belongs exclusively to your spouse above all others.

It's easy to understand this in relation to not becoming entangled in romantic interests. It's a little tougher to comprehend in regard to parents, children, relatives, and friends.

But how successful can a marriage be if one of the spouses always puts the interest of a child or a parent or a friend before the interests of their spouse? A marriage is a model of our relationship with Christ, who insists on our total and single-minded commitment to him.

Once married there is no other more important earthly relationship. Family members, friends, relatives, and acquaintances need to hold a far lesser place in your priorities than your spouse. Any time another relationship becomes a source of tension in a marriage, if the issue causing the tension cannot be reconciled, the relationship may need to be severed or at least distanced.

 Word from the Wise

"It is God's will that your good lives should silence those who make foolish accusations against you …. Show respect for everyone." (1 Peter 2:15-17)

Today it's believed that all respect has to be earned. This is not a biblical concept. The Bible commands that we are to respect everyone, because everyone is made in the image of God. This is especially true in families. Mutual respect is a given and not based on emotions or some point system.

Loving Respect

Paul concludes this passage by saying, "each man must love his wife as he loves himself, and the wife must respect her husband." Generally, women most crave love and security, while men primarily seek respect and admiration. Yet both desire all of these things and look for marriage to provide them.

You each bring talent, wisdom, experiences, knowledge, and more to the relationship. The makeup of these qualities will vary between you. While what you each bring may be different it is no less valuable. It's probably those differences that created a good deal of the initial attraction to one another.

It's also the differences that are frequent points of contention in marriage. In the heat of battle, respect gets tossed aside, along with selflessness, love, and all the other good stuff. Once the novelty of the wedding wears off, it's easy to lose sight of how charming and adorable our spouse's differences were. As more of reality takes over the marriage, those differences can seem more like nuisances than attractive qualities.

Yet, God has drawn you together to complement one another, not be mirror reflections. He has a purpose and a plan in mind for every couple. Before you knew each other, he knew each of you and gifted you both with varying talents and personalities that, when blended by his will, will yield tremendous fruit.

Learn to admire and cherish the differences in your mate. Seek to understand how what you each bring to the relationship can complement each other. Pray that God will allow you to see your spouse the way he sees them and to understand all the ways you both fit together.

Headship

There is one role that men are called to in a marriage that women are not. Just as some men insist on a warped view of submission, so some women (and men) misunderstand the concept of headship.

Calling the man to headship does not (a) put the woman in second place, or (b) give the man untethered authority to exert his will in the marriage. Both of these views ignore the context surrounding the verses on headship.

Being the head of a household or marriage is not about power or rights. It is about responsibility and everything else we've covered up to this point. In truth, it is a heavy and awesome responsibility that no man should take lightly or think of misusing. It is also something that a godly woman needs to understand.

Christ is the model for men in this role. Everything a godly man does or says as the head of his household and marriage needs to be measured against the example of Christ.

What does headship mean? It means prayerfully and humbly providing leadership, guidance, and direction in a marriage and a family in a fully responsible and accountable manner.

In most instances a husband and wife discuss decisions or courses of action and come to a mutually agreeable resolution. This will not always be possible. In these cases, it becomes the husband's responsibility to make a decision. This decision cannot be frivolous or made just to get his way. To meet the biblical requirements of headship, the husband must make a prayerful and even selfless decision that is within God's will and the best interests of the family.

Some of these decisions will be unbearably difficult. But the burden is lifted when his wife, even disagreeing, still loves, respects, and supports the husband's decision and course of action.

A misuse of headship can be seen in Jack. Jack, who has always wanted a boat, decided to go ahead and purchase one without his wife's knowledge, even though she has made it clear to him that it is not a purchase she agrees with. Another misuse of headship is Jack's making the purchase despite already being in debt on both cars and several other large household items. Jack's telling himself that he is the head of the house and he can buy a boat if he decides to, is not acting in the biblical headship Paul is describing. Purchasing the boat shows no regard or respect for his wife, and does not exhibit any responsibility. Definitely, it would be an act totally devoid of any input from the Holy Spirit!

In Jack-type situations a wife needs to stand her ground as the husband's decisions are to the detriment of the entire family. These types of decisions are not the ones where women submit to headship. These are the kinds of decisions where, if your husband doesn't listen to reason, you may need to go and speak with the pastor or elders of the church and have them intervene.

Another misuse of headship would be for a headstrong man to insist on his own way regardless of the misgivings or disagreement of his wife. This isn't biblical headship. Biblical headship is always exercised in consideration of and respect for the wife.

For Her

Being the head of one's house is tough duty and for any man who is honest with himself, intimidating. Likewise it can be scary feeling as if you are placing your life in the hands of your husband. If your husband is truly trying to do the right thing, he needs your love, respect, and support. He is bearing an awesome and heavy responsibility, having committed himself to always care for you and your children.

Another way for a wife to look at this situation is that she does not hold the same responsibility before God for her home and family. The buck stops with her husband and he is fully and totally accountable before God for everything that happens in your home. He will bear the brunt of God's wrath if things go awry. This is not your burden to carry before God.

An example of the proper use of headship might involve giving a donation to a ministry. Both a husband and wife sense the Holy Spirit encouraging them to give, yet the amount both have in mind is very different. Even after some discussion, they still fail to reach an agreement. In this situation, knowing that obedience to the Holy Spirit is critical, the husband must make a decision. The decision has nothing to do with his being right or wrong about the amount, but rather his best effort to comply with God's will.

Still considering his wife's point of view, the husband prayerfully seeks wisdom from the Holy Spirit as to what amount to give. When he is as certain as he can be that he has the mind of Christ, the husband writes the check and the wife accepts the decision. In the process of the man prayerfully seeking clarification regarding the amount, it is possible that the wife may have, on her own, come to the same decision as the man. It happens.

The amount may be more or less than what the wife wanted to give, and it may even be more or less than what the husband initially wanted to give. The point is that both sought to be obedient to God's prompting and the husband's final decision was made prayerfully, respectfully, and responsibly. This is the kind of situation where wives must yield to the decision of their husband.

If being "the head of the house" exhibits anything other than Christ-like behavior, then it is invalid and wrong. If, on the other hand, it exhibits loving consideration for one's wife and children, a passion for holiness, and a desire for nothing but God's best for all in the family, then it is headship as Paul and Jesus intended. A wife needs to accept her husband and love him and let go of her agendas in this type of circumstance.

Trust Is Hot

Only recently we've witnessed the repeated breaking of trust by corporate executives and, sadly, priests and other religious leaders. It's an all too common occurrence in politics, as well.

In marriage, as in any successful relationship, trust is a critical ingredient that seems easier to lose than sustain or regain.

How to Establish Trust

Before we can explore any aspect of trust, it's important to establish a definition. What is trust, anyway?

Trust, for a Christian, means being able to rely on the person in whom you have placed trust to do, say, or be what they say the will do, say, or be in the context of their being a Christian.

When you meet a person for the first time and discover they are a Christian, your trust level with that person goes up based on your shared faith. As you get to know them and learn that your belief systems are compatible, you will feel that you can rely on them to be honest, dependable, loving, and kind. You "trust" them to exhibit Christian behavior. You also trust them to maintain a holy thought life and healthy spirituality.

Trust Within Marriage

If, however, you hear them say or do something that is clearly contradictory to true Christianity, your trust level lowers. You don't necessarily become distrustful, but you are a bit more wary and cautious.

In marriage, trust issues can be volatile since the relationship between a husband and wife is so intimate. Trusting each other is crucial, especially when it comes to sexual issues.

The foundation of trust begins to be established from your first encounter and builds from there. You talk to each other, ask each other questions, and observe each other in various situations. Unfortunately, in the initial throes of love it's often easy to miss warning signs of trouble.

For example, a man says he is a Christian, is faithful to read his Bible, and attends church regularly. The woman takes him at his word. Yet, whenever they're together, he never brings up any topic related to faith, seldom talks about people he goes to church with, and, when she brings up faith, he quickly changes the subject. Taken in by his charm and other positive qualities, she may not make the connections that should cause a red flag to go up. In the context of their courting, they've gone to church together, she's seen his Bible (which does exhibit some wear), she's seen his personal library (which includes a few Christian books), and she's noticed that he has Christian CDs in his music collection. He doesn't swear, at least she's never heard him, and he's clean, healthy, and seems mature. She trusts him to be a Christian, but the trust is based on her assumptions more than on reality. Some people claim to be Christian because it's culturally acceptable and gains them advantages.

Word from the Wise

"And that is why I am suffering here in prison. But I am not ashamed of it, for I know the one in whom I trust, and I am sure that he is able to guard what I have entrusted to him until the day of his return." (2 Timothy 1:12)

Paul knew that he could trust Jesus Christ to guard what he had entrusted to him. We become trustworthy when we guard our loved one, when they can entrust themselves to us and be assured we will not betray them. When trust exists, love flourishes. When love flourishes, intimacy is sweet!

Once married, she begins to wonder. They go to his church but he's not particularly active and even makes excuses for missing Sunday services once or twice a month. She never sees him read his Bible and he always has an excuse for avoiding any kind of shared devotional or prayer time. At meals, he prays only if she insists. Something is out of whack and she starts to become distrustful.

The Dual Responsibility of Trust

In this scenario, who is responsible for the loss of trust? Both the husband and the wife. He's responsible for putting on a false front. She's responsible for not being more attentive to the signs that were there all along. Both will have work to restore trust. If nothing is done, the lack of trust the wife is experiencing will begin to broaden into other areas, even if it's not justified. She most likely will believe less and less of what he says, not count on him to do the things he promises, and soon both of them will be miserable.

In the beginning of any relationship, pay attention to ensure that the person in whom you are interested exhibits consistency and continuity between what they say and what they do. The scripture that says "by their fruits you shall know them" is a good measure. Likewise, be who you say *you* are.

Don't make promises you can't keep. Don't commit beyond what you're able to handle. Don't lead someone on if you're really not interested. Do what you say you are going to do. Be on time for dates. Be courteous and considerate.

Dr. Truth

"The two shall become one" develops not in bed but outside of bed. Any two people can have sex. That does not make them become "one." We become one when we can place the trust of our self into the hands of the other. When we do this together, at the same time, we become one. This can only occur when we provide the credence, the reliability, the truth, the honesty, and the dependability to our spouse so that they can rest safely in us.

How to Build Trust

So how do you build trust? By being trustworthy. By exhibiting faith, reliance, credence, dependence, honesty, and truthfulness, you build trust. This consistency can also be called godliness or Christian maturity.

What areas of marriage require both spouses to practice trustworthiness? Every area: handling and spending money, doing what you say you will do, being where you say you are, being a good parent to your children, consulting your spouse before consulting others, protecting marital information (finances, sexual practices, personal histories, and past sins), showing consideration for your spouse's thoughts and ideas, listening when your spouse needs you to listen, using sex as an expression of your love and trust, not as a weapon.

You also need to keep your expectations of each other realistic and balanced. It's unfair to withdraw your trust in someone over an issue they didn't realize was an expectation of yours. For example, in Susie's home growing up, her dad always initiated prayer before their evening meal. Susie mentioned this fact to Brad, and she knew Brad had observed it happening when he visited her family. When they were married, she expected Brad to initiate prayer before their evening meal just as her father did. In Brad's family, they didn't eat together in the evening; everyone fended for themselves.

When Brad didn't initiate prayer the first few weeks, Susie "reminded" him teasingly by joking about how she'd like him to pray. She figured he just needed a few weeks to adjust. When her "reminding" didn't work, she blew up. Brad was caught off guard. He had no idea that this was a serious expectation of hers. Since Brad's family hadn't observed this practice, he had no idea how important it was to Susie.

For Susie to infer from this that she couldn't trust Brad spiritually, or trust him to pray for her or their marriage, was a faulty deduction on her part. She had the responsibility to sit down with Brad and tell him how much this practice meant to her and to make a legitimate request that he do this at their meals. This would have engaged them both in a discussion about prayer in their marriage. They could have used this as a platform for further discussion.

Once Brad told Susie about his family history, Susie could see that he wasn't just trying to be a jerk—it was just not his custom. There was really no issue of trust here.

Brad and Susie's example may seem a little far-fetched, yet every relationship includes dozens of unrealized and unspoken expectations that each has of the other. As long as these expectations go undiscussed, no matter how trivial they may seem, trust will be eroded.

It's important to keep in mind that you and your spouse are human beings "prone to wander," or to commit sin. The only sinless person who ever walked the earth is Jesus. The rest of us are "sinless" only by God's grace and the applied blood of Jesus. We are, by our human nature, sinners through and through. We are incapable of living a sinless life. Praise be to God that because of his Son we can be "sinless" before him. In the meantime we have to deal with the fact that our sin has an effect on our spouse. We have to work overtime some days to deal with the pain, grieve the offense, confess our sins, and forgive each other so that we can climb out of the mess we've made and look forward to a new day tomorrow.

For Him

Your wife needs to know that you will turn to the Lord in times of marital strife. She needs to know that you will honestly come before God with your sin, that you will repent and that you will make amends. You need to confess your sin with her. Pray for her and with her every day. Pray for your marriage consistently and regularly. Spiritual trust and reliance on God should be a foundation in all Christian marriage.

One of the ways we establish trust is to face our foils, deal honestly with each other, and find a way to get past our hurdles together. Be consistent, be dependable, be truthful, be honest, and be respectful. If there is trouble, be humble, admit the truth, open your heart, and get help. How willing we are to deal with our own self when we mess up speaks volumes to our spouse. If we try to hide, if we try to cover-up, or if we try to lie there will be no trust.

Truth, truth, truth. What did Jesus say? "You are truly my disciples if you keep obeying my teachings. And you will know the truth, and the truth will set you free." (John 8:32) Truth sometimes hurts but hurt is reparable. Lies hurt worse and can be irreparable. At all times, speak the truth in love. Truth builds trust and the foundation of trust is obeying Christ's teachings.

How to Break Trust

How do you break trust with someone? You probably know more than 101 ways as you have both had your trust betrayed and broken trust with someone else. If you have ever broken a promise, no matter how trivial you thought it was, you betrayed someone else's trust in you.

Our first experiences being on the receiving end of broken trust happens when we are children. Parents, for any number of reasons, often tend to over promise and under deliver to their children, without meaning them any harm. Sometimes, a child perceives a promise when the parent is actually only speculating or saying maybe to something. A comment such as, "If we ever move to a farm, we'll get you a pony" is a conditional statement. However, a young child only hears "We'll get you a pony." When that never materializes, a sense of betrayal can haunt the child.

You betray the trusts of friends by promising to keep a shared piece of gossip confidential, and then sharing it with someone. All kinds of rationalizations come into play to justify your passing on the information, but the bottom line is that you have broken a trust.

In most instances, these relatively minor breaks in trust are healed and mended by apologies, clarification, or just the passing of time. In marriage, it gets a little more complicated.

The closer the person is to you, the more hurtful even a minor betrayal of trust can be. In marriage, every word and action tends to carry far more weight as each spouse "reads into" what the other is saying or doing. You each bring your own histories, cultures, memories, and more into the marriage. All of these elements color your perception of what your spouse does and says. This means that issues of trust can be perceived and interpreted differently.

Little things will happen between you because of these differences and you will both feel betrayed and hurt. However, these are actually the easiest trust issues to work through. A lot of patience coupled with a forgiving spirit and some clarifying discussion can usually clear things up.

Maintaining a forgiving spirit in marriage is absolutely essential for the health and survival of marriage. You are both going to hurt and offend each other to varying degrees throughout your marriage. It is inevitable because of the sinful nature that is always a part of us. Just as Christ is quick to forgive us our sins, you need to be quick to forgive the sins of your spouse. The pain of the breech of trust may take time to heal but we can't withhold forgiveness. "If another believer sins, rebuke him; but if he repents, forgive him. Even if he wrongs you seven times a day and each time turns again and asks forgiveness, forgive him." (Luke 17:3)

Sometimes forgiving gets really hard when the betrayal of trust seems especially egregious. A few examples of a serious break of trust include: emptying a bank account on a risky venture without telling your spouse, supporting a drug habit or sexual addiction, having an affair, never telling the truth about any number of things, sharing intimate and private secrets about your spouse with your friends, or even withholding important details about an event that your spouse has a right and need to know.

For Her

Forgiving an abusive husband does not come without your first getting to a place of safety and staying there. It is your husband's responsibility to provide you a safe home. No amount of forgiveness will fix abuse. If he is hurtful, he is hurtful. If he can't be trusted not to hurt you, he can't be trusted. Forgiveness can't be used to create the illusion of a healthy Christian marriage where abuse exists. You will know a loving man by his fruits; they may have a few little imperfections here and there but they aren't rotten!

How to Restore Trust

When the pain is small, trust is usually easily reclaimed. But when the hurt is huge, trust can seem shattered forever. It doesn't have to be. There is always hope and healing available through the help of the Holy Spirit.

While huge betrayals of trust may require time and effort to restore, they also require your willingness and decision to forgive. In fact, as Christians we are commanded to always forgive and seek restoration whenever possible. If your spouse has committed adultery, you are required to forgive him or her. If he or she wants to work to restore your marriage, you are required to work with him or her in counseling. You must make the honest effort, and allow the Holy Spirit to work with you both, to seek and find restoration. If both of you are truly committed to restoration, God will honor that and your marriage will be healed.

This is the case every time trust is broken. There must be repentance on the part of the spouse who broke trust, and there must be forgiveness on the part of the betrayed spouse. If both elements are present, healing is virtually guaranteed. How long it will take to restore trust depends on both spouses, but it must be restored to keep the marriage healthy.

It's very easy for the betrayed spouse to always look at their husband or wife with a jaundiced eye after a serious betrayal. This is understandable. But the goal must be to release the betrayal. This will happen over time as your spouse does not lapse back to their old sin and as you let go of your fear that another betrayal will occur. These things require both spouses to work hard for their marriage. We choose to forgive. We choose not to reengage in the behavior that broke our spouse's trust. It's a two-way street. Trust is both given and earned simultaneously.

The betrayer must become trustworthy. Repeatedly breaking trust will eventually break down a marriage completely. The spouse who is being betrayed need not accept abusive behavior that is repeated. If that is your situation, there may come a time when you forgive and then walk away. This is especially true if the betrayal involved dangerous or violent behavior that could put you and your children at risk. You need to leave and be safe.

For example, a husband is addicted to gambling and keeps gambling away the family's earnings. He has repeatedly apologized and promised to stop, even going to counseling for awhile. However, he continues to lie, gamble, and essentially steal the family's income. He may even become increasingly agitated each time he is confronted about his addiction. In this situation, no one is benefiting and trust is gone. The wife needs to either remove herself and her kids from the home or have the husband removed. The husband needs to be given an ultimatum to get help or lose his family. If he does indeed make an effort to get serious help, the wife needs to support and encourage him, but also hold him accountable over a long period of time before allowing him back into the family. She will need to work closely with the husband's therapist as they both work to restore trust and reunite the family. It can happen through the help of the Holy Spirit and a true willingness of the husband to make amends and get better.

In most instances, however, rebuilding trust does not follow an elaborate recovery plan that extends over months or years. It can happen in minutes, hours, days, or weeks. It requires both spouses choosing to trust and be trustworthy, as well as choosing to confess, repent, and forgive as needed.

If distrust lingers after reconciliation, a new wound is created. The one who was originally betrayed now becomes the betrayer. If you have extended true forgiveness to your spouse who has been genuinely repentant and is being trustworthy, yet you continue to harbor mistrust in your heart, you are living a lie and setting your spouse up for failure. Don't allow the enemy to cause you to live in fear. You will be robbed of joy at the same time.

Keep in mind, you both will betray each other's trust in big and small ways over the course of your marriage. It usually happens unintentionally, but not always. You are in need of your spouse's forgiveness and trust as much as they are in need of yours. Lay aside the grudge and allow the Holy Spirit to forgive through you so you can enjoy a peaceful and vital marriage.

How to Thrive In Trust

Trust is sexy. When you see your spouse being faithful, true, reliable, consistent, and considerate, you can't help but feel more attracted to him or her.

Watching your spouse deal with issues that involve you, to discover that they have talked about you in a way that esteems you, touches the heart very deeply. Hearing your spouse talk about you with devotion and integrity leaves you feeling secure and safe. Even if you overhear them a few times you know that this is the way they talk about you. It leaves you knowing you can trust what they tell other people about you.

When husbands and wives know through experience with their spouses that they are safe, guarded, and protected, love grows, love deepens. It's also a turn-on!

Men will tell you that when their wife has their genitals in her hands it is a moment of ultimate trust. To surrender his sexual organs to his wife is one of the greatest acts of trust he will ever engage in.

When women open their legs and let their husbands come in, they are opening their entire soul. The moment of orgasm is a moment of total surrender of the self. It is a moment of total ecstasy when shared with a man who has her trust.

Together we surrender our hearts, our minds, our souls, and our bodies to each other. The moment of orgasm is the moment in life that we are the most vulnerable. Sex within marriage creates the perfect environment for our vulnerability to be guarded and cared for. This is why Father God tells us not to share our sexuality with anyone other than the one who has entered a covenant with us. It is the marriage covenant that was created to care for us, protect us, nurture us, and allow us to bear our greatest vulnerabilities. In a similar way, we surrender our souls to God, being vulnerable and trusting him to protect us and not doing things our own way. This is how we can know true oneness with him.

Trust. A trustworthy spouse becomes the person with whom we can truly bare our entire soul.

 ## Word from the Wise

"Since I was so sure of your understanding and trust, I wanted to give you a double blessing." (2 Corinthians 1:15)

The Apostle Paul gives us a realistic idea of how we feel when we know we can trust someone deeply. We want to give them a double blessing. Wives, husbands, if you want the best possible marriage and a great sex life, be understanding and trustworthy. From there sexual intimacy can become the sweetest thing you'll ever know this side of heaven!

Chapter 21

Faithfulness Is Fulfilling

Faithfulness involves more than just sex. It encompasses trust, respect, loyalty, and more. Just like love, faithfulness is a choice, or rather a series of choices, made daily. The results of faithfulness are worth the effort.

Being Truly One

When you first get married, you probably have some romantic notion of what "being one" means. You know it has something to do with sex, but even then the details of how it works are sketchy. Yet, you believe that the magic will take over and this oneness thing will naturally happen once the vows are spoken.

But reality soon breaks up your illusion. You may make it through the honeymoon and even the first months of marriage before you begin to realize that you don't have a clue as to what this oneness thing is all about! Where's the magic?

In all of the preaching done in pulpits, in the Sunday school classes, in the talks parents give their kids about sex, and in all the sex education in schools, it is doubtful you will find any reference to oneness, let alone any how-to tips. At best, if you hear any mention of oneness in these venues, it will be in a way that feeds the romantic notions instead of offering practical instruction.

So what is oneness? It does not mean that your personalities merge into a single blob of sameness. Nor does it mean that from the moment you say "I do" that your every decision will be shared in perfect mutual harmony. In marriage, you will retain your distinct personalities and will find endless issues that will spark heated and intense discussion.

So what is the dish on oneness? D.I.S.H. is it! Oneness involves Desire, Intentions, Soul, and Heart.

Desire

Oneness starts with desire. When you were alone, you desired to be in relationship with another. When you met that special one, you developed a deep desire to be with them. When you shared wedding vows, you wrapped your desire in commitment to that one person and they to you. Your initial desire was to be in unity in an exclusive mutually loving relationship with one special person for the rest of your life. This is the beginning of oneness.

Desire is something that ebbs and flows in your marriage over time. You can encourage it by taking moments here and there to ponder your spouse, recall the nice things they have done for you, think about their commitment to you, think of some of the qualities that drew you to them when you met, and think of something playful you did together. We mentioned earlier that sex starts in the mind with a thought. Desire can start with loving thoughts toward your spouse. As you ponder your spouse, you'll become aware of how much your heart starts to long for them. From the depths of your heart you may also notice your soul yearning for your spouse.

Sexual intimacy is not the goal here. While this may happen, it shouldn't be expected every time you think loving thoughts of your spouse. You can use that moment to think of something loving you can do for your spouse, to think of something you need to apologize for, or just to relish the fact that he or she chose you! Of all the people in the world, he or she chose you!

Intentions

Marriage states the intention of you and your spouse to be united together. Together you form a new family. Together you speak in agreement, or one voice, on many things. Together, you stand before the world and declare your intention to be loyal, faithful, and devoted to one person, your spouse. Your intention is to act together as one unit, as husband and wife.

We reinforce our oneness when we say to someone who has invited us to do something, "I'll check with my spouse about that and I'll get back to you." This message tells people that you are not a solo entity, that your spouse is part of your life and that their opinion, idea, or availability is important to you. When people ask you to be involved in church ministry and you say, "My spouse and I will pray about that and I'll get back to you," you're doing two things—you are letting people know that you operate as a team, and you are respecting your spouse's thoughts and opinions on activities that affect your family.

Our primary intention toward our spouse—to act in concert with them—is not just a thought or a feeling, but an outward expression by which we remind others that we don't operate independent of our spouse.

Acting as a unit ought not to be an oppressive or controlling issue on the part of one spouse. Ephesians 5 tells spouses to submit themselves to each other. We lay our intentions, desires, hopes, and dreams before our spouse. We seek their input. We act in unison. We do not make unilateral decisions that disrespect and devalue the voice of our spouse. One spouse insisting that the other do what they want is not oneness—it is an attempt at control and domination.

Soul

Marriage is a holy institution and a holy state of being. As you and your spouse commit to each other before God, God in turn allows your hearts and souls to intermingle. This aspect of marriage truly is magical. As you both grow and mature as Christians together, your soul's deep desires, intentions, and communion with God become more and more intertwined. You are able to sense and perceive by the Holy Spirit how to love and care for each other in an incredibly intimate manner. You feel, in your soul, unified.

 Word from the Wise

"As the scriptures say, 'A man leaves his father and mother and is joined to his wife, and the two are united into one.' This is a great *mystery*, but it is an illustration of the way Christ and the church are one. So again I say, each man must love his wife as he loves himself, and the wife must respect her husband." (Ephesians 5:32-33)

Paul acknowledged that the spiritual oneness that Christ has with his church (the covenant of God with his people) is illustrated in the love between man and woman in marriage.

There are a miniscule number of relationships we will have in our lives where we feel the connection of our soul. Women with a mother's heart feel this toward their children. Fathers can develop this feeling for their children. Depending on the way we were mothered or fathered we may feel this with our parents. Part of this connection with our family is biological, but the other comes with love.

With your spouse there is no biological connection like this. And, most of the time, you and your spouse don't have years of history together before you get married. The soul connection is a mystical connection that forms between husband and wife over a lifetime. It begins during courting and engagement and is sealed after the wedding and sexual union. But it's not over then and it hasn't yet become all it can be.

Just as a father develops this kind of connection with his children through pouring out his self-sacrificing love to them, we develop oneness with our spouse through pouring ourselves out in loving self-sacrifice toward them. No matter how much bonding there is between parent and child, that bond will never reach the kind of oneness that Christian men and women can attain in marital union. Nothing, absolutely nothing on earth comes close to this union of souls.

Heart

In marriage, you exchange hearts. You each entrust the other with the care and nurturing of your own heart. This is a willful act, and has nothing to do with chemistry or fate. As you grow in love (it doesn't stop on the wedding day!) you become more aware of the heart of your mate and how much of their life is dependent upon and devoted to you.

As we trust our spouses to care for our heart and see that they are trustworthy, we entrust even more of ourselves in our spouse. As our spouse continues to respond in love and consideration of us, the depth of trust continues to deepen. How sweet it is to rest in each other, to feel safe in each other.

When there is conflict with our spouse we hold our hearts at bay for a short time but as confession, repentance, and forgiveness wash over the conflict we decide again to trust our spouse. We recognize that they are human. We recognize that we are human. That marriage brings its pains and joys and it's all part of life.

All together, these elements are what make up oneness in marriage. The practical aspects of supporting oneness are discussed throughout this book. Becoming one involves good, healthy sex, as well as trust, respect, and holiness before the Lord.

You can be one while agreeing to disagree and even in the midst of a knockdown, superheated, verbal fistfight! In a sense, this magical thing does occur naturally over time, but only as you work on the aspects of having a good marriage. It does not develop without effort. Yet as it grows, it serves as the reinforcement and undergirding of your marriage. It serves as a source of strength, certainty, and peace even in the midst of temporary marital strain and discord.

Word from the Wise

"I am not worthy of all the faithfulness and unfailing love you have shown to me, your servant." (Genesis 32:10)

Faithfulness results from unfailing love, and love is a choice. Let God's unfailing love flow through you and into your marriage. Nurture it daily in the grace of God.

Glances versus Stares

One of the more obvious and pervading threats to oneness is marital unfaithfulness. In marriage, it too often seems as if the grass is always greener everywhere else! You get married and the romance wears off, the novelty of your new bride or groom fades, there seems to be more battle than bliss, you begin to envy your still single friends, and that hunk next door or hottie at work keeps popping into your thoughts.

It's known that men are more visually oriented than women and just catching a glance of a sexy female can put a man's libido in gear. A common caution given to men is to avoid letting the glance turn into a stare.

This is a good caution for both the husband and wife. Sexual unfaithfulness, by both husbands and wives, has devastated thousands of marriages. In every instance, a glance was allowed to become a stare, which led to action.

You can see things with your eyes and with your imagination. A glance can be visual, or it can be the thought that passes through your mind. Both men and women can become sexually aroused visually and, if the arousal becomes desire, adultery can be the result. Stop your mind from creating any pictures of being sexually or romantically involved with the person you find attractive.

Usually, though, sexual arousal will not be the only or primary factor in adultery. A woman may become disillusioned with her marriage and begin to fantasize about a new romantic relationship with another, "better" man. The fantasy isn't about sex, but is rooted in a desire for what she perceives is missing from her marriage. Or she could have an immature attitude toward marriage and be unwilling to take on her own responsibility to work at making things better. Men will be drawn to another woman for the same reasons.

Marriage brings with it joy and pain, trust and betrayal, satisfaction and anger, and a host of other conflicting emotions and experiences. Successful couples are successful not because their marriages are free from challenges, but because they have remained faithful to their commitment to work toward oneness rather than run from problems.

Unfortunately, because two individuals are involved in a marriage, it is entirely possible for one to destroy the marriage. A husband may be fully committed to his wife, remaining faithful, working hard, willing to go to counseling, and doing everything within his power to make the marriage stronger, yet his wife is determined to leave. In a situation where one has willfully and determinedly set their desires, intentions, soul, and heart away from their marriage toward another person or situation, there is little hope of reconciliation.

It is possible for a person to become so fixated on "greener grass" that it becomes for them the only solution. We each have free will and even God does not force us to remain faithful to him; it's a choice we have to make. It is tragic and painful to have a spouse turn away, but it is their choice no matter how unfair it seems.

For Him

Your eyes *will* wander. This is inevitable. But beware when your eyes fixate! Be aware of what's going through your head and your heart. You might not be able to keep from looking when a sexy woman walks by, but you can control how long you look. And you can control what you think about as you're looking. If you catch yourself looking too long and for the wrong reasons, turn around and walk the other way for a minute or so. If you're with your wife, look at her and give her a hug.

When the Mind Wanders

"Prone to wander, Lord I feel it!" That is our nature in relationship with God and that is our nature in relationship with marriage and many other situations. Turning away from a challenge or even an opportunity that involves effort and risk always seems an easier choice. How can you manage your tendency to wander, especially when it comes to your marriage?